Beginning Autoharp Instruction Book

Bonnie Phipps

Here are some unique features of this book:
- Students will learn many different strumming patterns.
- Students will learn how to use the low, middle and high areas of the strings effectively.
- Each strumming pattern is presented first in a chord progression "exercise" and then in a song.
- The book helps the student find logical left hand finger positions on the chord bars.
- Appendix A has a section on "Playing Simple Songs by Ear."
- Appendix B covers tuning, stringing, refelting, cleaning the Autoharp, and ordering parts.

Dick Carter, Wilmington, Delaware

John *Kilby* Snow

Dedication

Kilby Snow (May 28, 1905 to March 20, 1980)

This book is dedicated to John *Kilby* Snow. He began playing the Autoharp® * at the early age of four. He loved the Autoharp with all his heart and became one of the greatest Autoharp players in the history of the instrument.

Acknowledgments

Special thanks and love to my dear mother, Arlene Phipps, who typed all of my manuals. Also to Diane Hesse, Patty Ortise Wright and Mary Nicholass. Lastly, to Bob Peterson, for his marvelous photographs.

Instruction Tape

To help you learn faster and easier, Bonnie Phipps has put together an instruction cassette tape that corresponds to the strum patterns and songs in this book. To order a tape send an $8.00 check or money order to:

Bonnie Phipps Instruction Tape
P.O. Box 9656
Denver, Colo. 80209

Biography

Bonnie Phipps is among a handful of accomplished Autoharp players who have tapped undeveloped potentials of the instrument. National Autoharp champion of 1982, Kicking Mule recording artist and contributor to *FRETS* music magazine, Bonnie is quickly gaining national recognition. Ms. Phipps, a former school teacher, performs for children as well as adults and is involved in the Colorado "Artist in Residence" program. She conducts workshops on the Autoharp, children's songs and storytelling for music organizations, festivals, colleges and public schools.

*Autoharp is the registered trade name of Oscar Schmidt-International in the United States and Canada.

2

Bonnie Phipps

Larry Laszlo

Preface

The inspiration for this book comes from my love of the Autoharp and my enthusiasm for teaching. I remember when I first began playing the instrument in 1971, I was so excited. I discovered that on the Autoharp, I could make music right away! Working with the Autoharp and teaching myself what the instrument can do is a joyful process. I hope I can help you discover some of that joy.

I have written this book for beginners. It teaches you, step by step, about the instrument and music. You will learn a variety of strumming techniques, to work the chord bars, to use the different areas of the strings effectively, and to play songs and simple melodies. And that is only the beginning . . .

Enjoy,

Bonnie Phipps

Bonnie Phipps

For Autoharp Teachers

The techniques that are developed in this book will provide a good foundation for advanced study. As a beginner's book, its primary focus is on developing coordination of the right hand by presenting a variety of strumming patterns from simple to complex. I suggest that those students who are new to music work through this book in the order it is written, along with any supplemental material you wish to provide.

Some students who are already familiar with music (especially those who have played guitar) can begin to learn melody picking at the same time as they are learning strumming techniques. As teacher to teacher, let me wish you the best, and I hope you and your students enjoy using this book.

For School Teachers

Autoharps can be found in most elementary schools. Since many children's songs use only two or three chords, you can begin using the instrument in the classroom right away. Another plus feature is that Autoharps are portable, which allows you to play closer to the children. You can teach children to play as well. While this book is not geared specifically to teaching children, you can easily adapt it to fit their needs. It works best when children play standing up with the Autoharp on a table about waist level. Fingerpicks are not necessary until the children begin playing melody. I suggest they use a flat pick at first to play the rhythms. Just follow the direction of the arrows in the exercises and away we go!

History of the Autoharp

The Autoharp is one of the few instruments that is native to the United States. Its history began when Charles F. Zimmerman, a renowned accordion player and builder from Germany, created a new musical notation system. After years of struggle, in vain, to introduce his "Tone Number System," he decided to build an instrument that would help teach his new method. In 1881, after two years of experimentation, he perfected the Autoharp. It was a cross between a zither (a German instrument) and an accordion; similar in shape and size to a zither and in chord structure to the accordion. This newly created instrument was played laying flat on a person's lap or on a table with the chord bars facing them. The strings were strummed at the bottom part of the instrument near the bridge. At that time, the music of the Autoharp was mainly arpeggios made by graceful swoops across the strings.

Autoharps were made and sold only in the East until the early 1900's when it was brought to the South by door-to-door teacher/salesmen. These salesmen would teach people to play, hire an auditorium for them to play in, and then take orders for more Autoharps at the performance. The southern people responded to the Autoharp and soon it became a part of their traditional music. Not content with the original "harp-like" sound, the people of the southern mountains evolved their own style, heavily influenced by traditional "Old Timey" guitar and banjo techniques. This style consists of plucking melody notes with the first finger and strumming occasionally with the thumb.

It wasn't until around 1940 that people started playing them like they teach in schools, with one hand crossed over. Maybelle Carter, one of the famous country music group called "The Carter Family," discovered that the Autoharp sounded better when she crossed her right hand over her left and strummed the strings on the top half of the instrument. She later found that holding the instrument upright freed her from the need of a table and gave her better mobility to play. This upright position has become very popular today.

Until recently, the Autoharp's musical potential has remained relatively unrecognized. Its main attraction has been as an educational tool used in the schools, or as a novelty rather than as a serious musical instrument. Currently, a handful of accomplished players are demonstrating the instrument's capabilities to produce dynamic expressions, varied tones, rhythmic movements, melodic sequences and embellishments within a variety of styles and techniques. They are playing Bach, chorales, fiddletunes note-for-note, ragtime, jazz, and other forms of music once thought impossible on the Autoharp. These players have had to teach themselves what they know through experimenting and discovering new ways of playing. As they have tapped undeveloped potentials of the instrument, they have also created new challenges for Autoharp players.

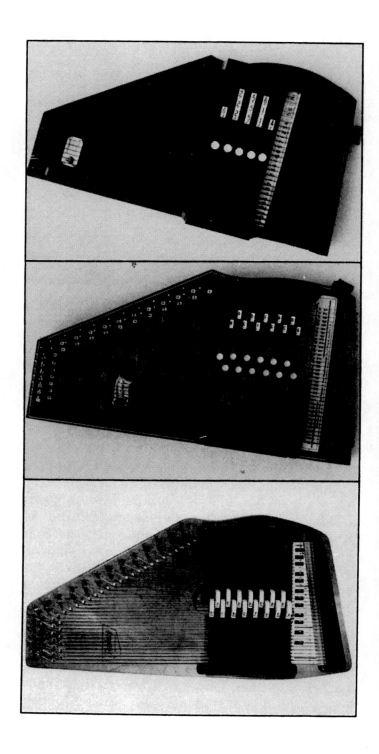

Contents

Introduction

Figure 1 is a diagram of a 15-bar Autoharp. Its individual parts are named and numbered.

1. Chord Bars	5. String Guide
2. Chord Buttons	6. Strings
3. Bar Carriage	7. Bridge
4. Tuning Peg	8. Sound Hole

The Autoharp's strings range in order from the lowest bass F (two octaves below middle C), to the highest C (two octaves above middle C). The strings fall roughly into four octaves: bass, low, middle and high. When a chord bar is pressed, the felt on the bottom of the bar mutes (silences) certain strings while allowing others to sound. For example, if the F major chord bar is pressed, only the notes in that chord, in this case F, A and C, will ring.

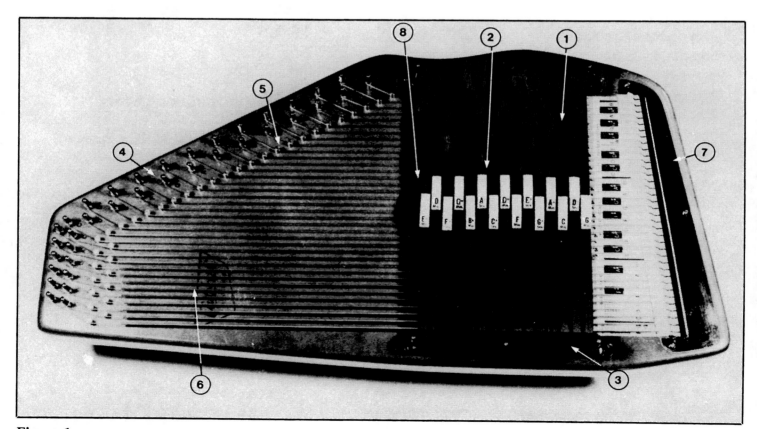

Figure 1.

HOLDING THE AUTOHARP:

There are two basic ways to hold the Autoharp. In the traditional position, the musician holds the Autoharp flat in his lap (Figure 2a), or on a table (Figure 2b) with the chord bars facing him. The left hand works the chord bars and the right hand crosses over the left hand and strums the strings left of the bars, or strums the strings to the right of the bar. The right elbow is raised slightly. It wasn't until the late 40's that the Autoharp began to be played in an upright position, a method first developed by Maybelle Carter. In this method, you hold the Autoharp in a light embrace with one corner on your left leg, and with the back resting against your left shoulder (Figure 3). The left hand is in position to work the chord bars; the left wrist should be bent with the fingertips resting comfortably and lightly on the chord buttons. Keep your left elbow down so that your arm is out of the way of the upper register strings. The right arm steadies the Autoharp and the right hand plays rhythm and melodies on the strings.

I suggest holding the instrument in the upright position because it gives the right hand more freedom of movement. The chord bars cannot be as easily seen in this position, but you will soon learn to rely more on touch than on visual cues. The upright position has a further advantage — it allows the Autoharp player to play standing up. The Autoharp can be fitted with a strap by placing one strap button on the side about opposite the middle octave G peg, and another on the opposite side near the bridge plate.

Figure 2a.

Figure 2b.

Figure 3.

Introduction

FINGERPICKS:

If you want to play with other musicians, you will need the extra volume fingerpicks provide to hold your own against other louder instruments. Fingerpicks also protect your fingers and allow you to produce a wider variety of sounds from your Autoharp.

You will need both thumb and fingerpicks of either metal or plastic. It is a good idea to buy a variety at first. Experiment with combinations until you find the type which pleases you. Metal picks give a bright sound, plastic picks have a softer tone.

The picks should be comfortable but snug; they should not slide on your finger when you play. Put the fingerpicks on and then push the tips against a hard surface to force them tightly down on to the fingers. The tip of the picks should be about one-quarter inch above the fingertips. The thumbpick should be worn approximately in the middle of the thumb-nail (Figure 4).

You can also use flat picks of either plastic or felt. They are held between the thumb and first knuckle of the index finger (Figure 5). These picks work well for accompaniments but not as well for playing melody.

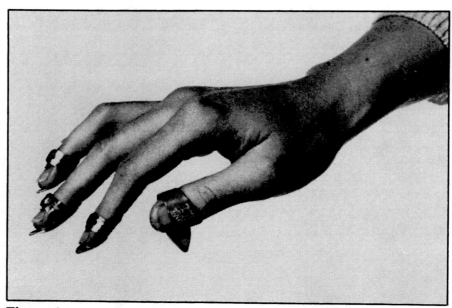

Figure 4.

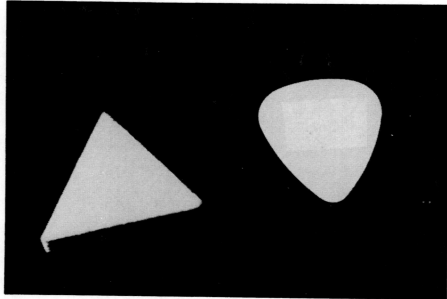

Figure 5.

Beginning Strumming Techniques

In this chapter you will learn to strum a variety of rhythm patterns and to use these strums to accompany songs. You will also learn to work the chord bars. You only need to know a few basic music principles to begin playing the Autoharp. Appendix A on *Basic Music Theory* (page 75) will help you understand the musical terms in this book. If you do not have a musical background, I suggest you read pages 75 to 78 of that section before continuing this chapter.

The strums in this chapter are used first in chord progressions* rather than songs. This is so you can concentrate on the strums and not be confused by words and melodies which usually have a different rhythm than the strum patterns. Pete Seeger writes in his book, *How To Play the Five String Banjo,* that it is more important for the beginner to concentrate on rhythm than on melody. He says that the banjo player's right hand (and the Autoharp player's as well) must. . . "learn each pattern of strumming and picking so well that he doesn't even need to think about it. Then if he wants to sing a song, he can concentrate on the song without worrying about the details."

---

*A chord progression is a series of chords that usually makes up a song (see Appendix A).

Here are a few suggestions that may help as you are learning each strumming pattern. First, clap out the rhythm patterns of each strum; it will be much easier to play if you are familiar with how it sounds (see the Clapping Exercises on page 78 of Appendix A). Second, press any major chord button and strum the rhythm pattern without changing chords (try singing one-chord songs as you strum, such as *Kookaburra, Row Your Boat,* or *Farmer in the Dell*). When this feels comfortable, play the chord progression in the exercise.

Once a rhythm feels natural with the chord progression, use it to accompany a simple song. I suggest, at first, a song that has no more than three chords. Section B in this chapter provides a variety of songs that you can use to practice your new techniques. There are also a number of songbooks written for Autoharp (see page 88).

SECTION A

LEFT HAND

When you play a song, you want to find the most comfortable and economical finger patterns for your left hand. Most Autoharp players will rest their fingers lightly on the three or four main chord bars used in a song. Their fingers remain in that position throughout the song. Occasionally they may play other chords, but their fingers always return to the original position. This establishes a "home base" (similar to the home position in typing) and helps you to memorize the chord positions in each key. Chord buttons should be pressed firmly. Keep the pressure steady and let up on one button just as you press down on another. For players who hold the Autoharp upright, there will be a section on "Left Hand Finger Positions" for most of the exercises. This will help you to find logical finger patterns on the chord bars without looking. Each Autoharp player has a slightly different approach. The finger positions I have given are only suggestions; they are what work best for me.

Beginning Strumming Techniques

TABLATURE

The symbols (also called Tablature) for the right hand are as follows: ↑ — Strike the strings in a motion towards the high register strings. You can use either your thumb (Figure 6a) or your finger(s) (Figure 6b). I suggest you use your thumb, especially when you are striking the lower register strings. If you use your finger(s), hold them at a slight angle as you strum toward the higher register. This helps to avoid getting them caught in the strings.

↓ — Strike the strings in a motion towards the lower register strings (Figure 7). Use your finger(s) only.

Before you begin the strumming exercises, practice pressing the chord buttons and strumming across the strings. For example, firmly press the F major chord bar with your middle or index finger. Strum across the strings several times with your thumb. Keep your wrist loose and your elbows raised slightly; create an arc-like movement as your thumb moves quickly across the strings (Figure 8). On the next page are two songs to help you become familiar with the strumming and pressing the chord bars.

Figure 6a.

Figure 6b.

Figure 7.

Figure 8.

Frère Jacques uses only one chord. The time signature is 4/4, so you will count 1-2-3-4, 1-2-3-4, etc. Press the C chord bar and strum across the strings on the first and third count of each measure.

FRÈRE JACQUES

HINT: The first note you sing is C. If you are having trouble hearing where to begin singing, pluck the C note on the Autoharp.

Skip To My Lou uses two chords, F and C7. The time signature is 4/4. Again, you will strum on the first and third beat of each measure. You change from the F chord to the C on the first beat of the third measure. Try to keep a steady beat as you change chords.

SKIP TO MY LOU

Beginning Strumming Techniques

STRUM PATTERNS

For the following exercises in this chapter, the strings are divided into two sections (low and high) (Figure 9a). Occasionally they are divided into three sections (low, middle and high) (Figure 9b). You will use different combinations of these sections to play your rhythm patterns. The same rhythm played in just one area of the strings will sound different when you combine the high and low areas to play it.

Figures 10a and 10b show how we will indicate which sections of the strings you are to play. The placement of the tablature indicates whether you are to strum in the low, middle, or high sections of the strings. Notice that the note value of each symbol and the corresponding count is written directly below the symbols.

Figure 10.

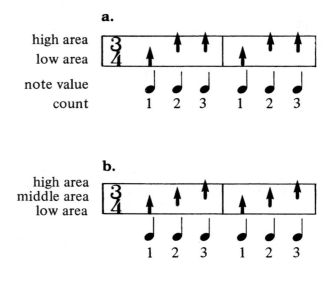

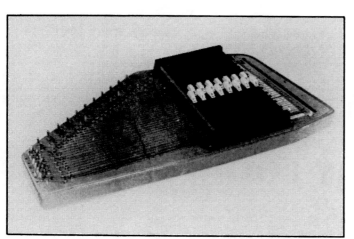

Figure 9a.

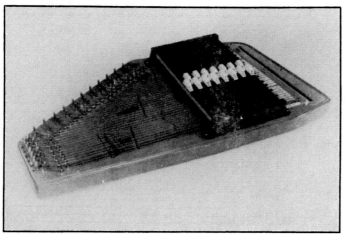

Figure 9b.

Now let's look at Exercise 1. The first chord you are to push is F. The time signature is 4/4. On the first count, strike the low area of the strings; on the second count, strike the high area; on the third count, again strike the low area; and then strike the high area on the fourth count. This process is repeated for each measure. You change from the F chord to the C chord on the first count of the third measure. The symbol :‖ at the end of the measure means to go back to the beginning and repeat the sequence. Repeat each exercise many times until your hand feels coordinated and you no longer have to look at the symbols to play the rhythm, but feel and hear the rhythms naturally.

EXERCISE 1

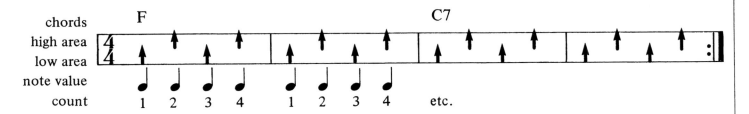

Finger Positions

12-15 Bar Autoharp — Press the F chord bar with the middle finger and the C7 chord bar with the index finger.

21 Bar Autoharp — Press the F chord bar with the middle finger and the C7 chord bar with the index finger.

Suggested Practice Songs

Mary Ann, page 29 (A)

Buffalo Gals, page 30 (B)

Exercise 2 is a variation of Exercise 1 in 3/4 (waltz) time.

EXERCISE 2

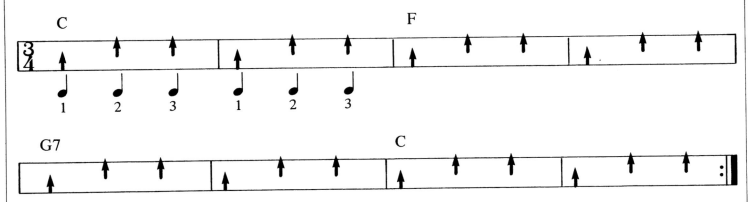

Finger Positions In the beginning, it is a natural tendency for students to use their first three fingers to press the chord bars and ignore the thumb. The thumb is most instrumental in allowing your fingers to cover a wide range of movements. I suggest you use it from the very beginning.

Rest your fingers lightly on all three chords that are to be played. Keep your fingers in that position as you play the chord progression. This type of "centering" around the main chords in a song (or exercise) can be used in everything you play.

12-15 Bar Autoharp — Your middle finger is centered on C, your index finger on G7 and your thumb on F.

21 Bar Autoharp — Your ring finger rests on C, your index finger on G7 and your thumb on F. This frees your middle finger to work the minor chords.

Suggested Practice Songs

Clementine, page 31 (C)

Down In the Valley, page 32 (D)

Beginning Strumming Techniques

In Exercises 3 and 4 you will be using the low, middle, and high areas of the strings.

EXERCISE 3

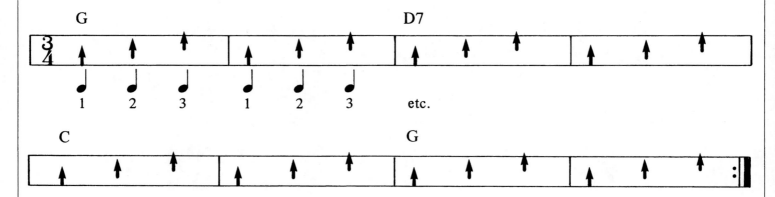

etc.

Finger Positions

12-15 Bar Autoharp — The middle finger rests on the G, the ring finger on D7, and the index finger on the C.

21 Bar Autoharp — The ring finger rests on G, the index finger on D7 and the thumb on C.

Suggested Practice Songs

Down In the Valley, page 32 (D)

My Bonnie, page 33 (E)

EXERCISE 4

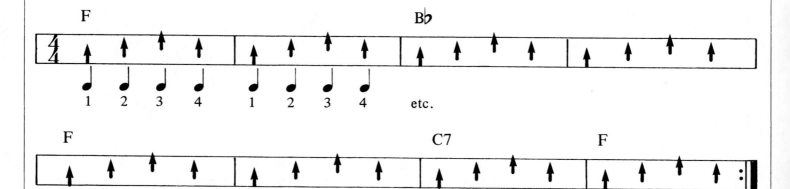

etc.

Finger Positions

12-15 Bar Autoharp — The middle finger rests on the F, the index finger on C7 and the thumb on Bb.

21 Bar Autoharp — The ring finger rests on F, the index finger on C7 and the thumb on Bb.

Suggested Practice Songs

Mary Ann, page 29 (A)

Oh Susanna, page 34 (F)

Remember to press the chord buttons firmly. If your sound is not clear, it may mean you are not pressing hard enough.

DOUBLE STRUMMING

In Exercises 5 and 6, you will strike the strings in a back and forth motion (↑ ↓). I call this *double strumming*. Some Autoharp players move only their fingers back and forth over the strings, keeping them at a slight angle. Other players, myself included, use their thumb and finger(s) alternately to strike the strings. It is important to keep your wrist loose and your fingers curved (Figure 11). The movement is similar to shaking your hand back and forth with a very loose wrist.

The rhythm of Exercise 5 is made up of eighth notes, so the count is 1 & 2 & 3 & 4 &. If you were to tap the beat of the exercise with your foot, it would tap the floor directly on the counts 1-2-3-4, and come off the floor between each count on the &. It is called the *downbeat* when your foot taps the floor, and the *upbeat* when your foot comes off the floor. The symbols are tied together when they occur within one beat. For example, ↑↓ . The first beat of each measure is accented (>). This means to strike the strings harder.

EXERCISE 5

G · · · · · · · Amin

$\frac{4}{4}$ ↑↓ ↑↓ ↑↓ ↑↓ | ↑↓ ↑↓ ↑↓ ↑↓ | ↑↓ ↑↓ ↑↓ ↑↓ | ↑↓ ↑↓ ↑↓ ↑↓

1 & 2 & 3 & 4 &   1 & 2 & 3 & 4 &   etc.
>   >

C · · · · · · · G

↑↓ ↑↓ ↑↓ ↑↓ | ↑↓ ↑↓ ↑↓ ↑↓ | ↑↓ ↑↓ ↑↓ ↑↓ | ↑↓ ↑↓ ↑↓ ↑↓ :||

Finger Positions

12-15 Bar Autoharp — Your middle finger rests on G and your index finger on C. Your thumb plays A minor.

21 Bar Autoharp — Your ring finger rests on G and your thumb on C. Your middle finger plays the A minor. The middle finger is good at working the bottom two rows of chords.

Suggested Practice Songs

Buffalo Gals, page 30 (B)

Down By the Riverside, page 36 (G)

Figure 11.

Roz Brown and John McCutcheon

15

Beginning Strumming Techniques

EXERCISE 6

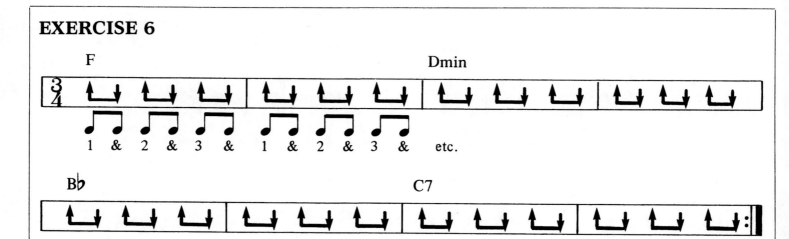

Finger Positions

12-15 Bar Autoharp — The middle finger rests on the F, the index finger on the C7, the thumb on B♭ and the ring finger plays D minor. The ring finger is especially agile at working the back row of chords.

21 Bar Autoharp — The ring finger rests on F, the index finger on C7, the thumb on B♭ and the middle finger plays D minor.

Suggested Practice Songs

Clementine, page 31 (C)

Beautiful, Beautiful, Brown Eyes, page 37 (H)

In the following exercises, you will combine the single strokes and double strums in a variety of ways to produce different rhythm patterns. Exercise 7 is similar to Exercise 1. You are merely adding a downward stroke after the second and fourth beat.

EXERCISE 7

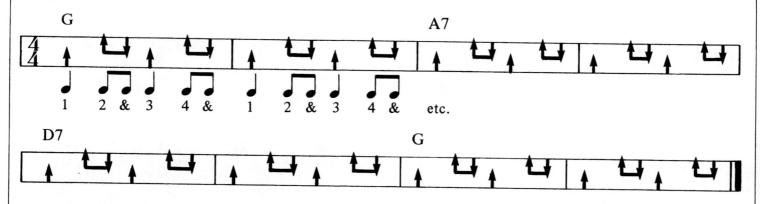

Finger Positions

12-15 Bar Autoharp — Your middle finger rests on G, your ring finger on D7, and your thumb on A7.

21 Bar Autoharp — Your ring finger rests on G, your index finger on D7, and your middle finger on A7.

Suggested Practice Songs

Oh Susanna, page 34 (F)

Rock-A My Soul, page 38 (I)

EXERCISE 8

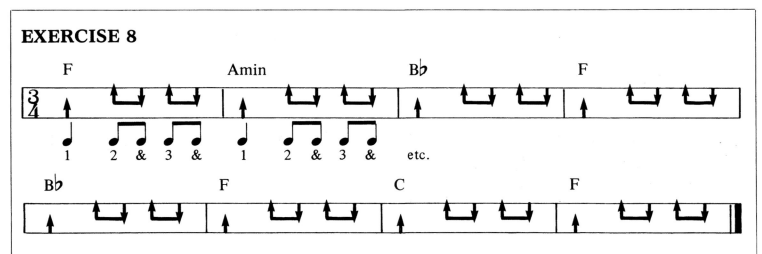

Finger Positions

12-15 Bar Autoharp — Your thumb rests on B♭, your index finger on F, and your middle finger on C. Your ring finger plays A minor.

21 Bar Autoharp — Your thumb rests on B♭, your index finger on F, and your middle finger on C. Use your ring finger for A minor.

HINT: As you are pressing the F chord bar in the first measure, your ring finger is reaching toward the A minor.

Suggested Practice Songs

My Bonnie, page 33 (E)

Daisy Bell, page 39 (J)

Now you are ready to begin experimenting with the sounds the instrument can produce. Different tones are created by the way your fingers touch the strings. You can strike the strings lightly or with more force, depending on the feelings you want to express during certain parts of a song. The number of strings you strum can vary the sounds. For instance, strum over a three-inch area of the strings and then strum over a larger area. The bass section may sound mushy on some of the chords. You can compensate by striking the strings a little higher in pitch.

The variety of fingers used in your strumming also varies the sound quality. Try using three fingers in your rhythms and then try just one finger. Compare the difference. Try alternating your index, middle, and ring fingers with your thumb as you are double strumming. For example, in Exercise 5, use your index finger after the first beat, middle finger after the second, ring finger after the third, then middle after the fourth. Each finger will strike a slightly different area of the strings to create a pattern of higher and lower sounds. The orders in which you can alternate your fingers are numerous.

You can use combinations of the low, middle and high areas of the strings to create a variety of effects. Here are some ideas:

• Take a rhythm pattern from an earlier exercise but instead of using all the strings, play it in the high area only, separating that area into two or three sections.

• Divide the low area of the Autoharp into two sections. As you stroke in the lower octave, alternate your thumb strokes between the lowest strings and a few strings higher. This is called an *alternating bass*. For example, to alternate the bass in Exercise 7, strike the lowest strings on the first beat and strike a few strings higher on the third beat, but stay in the lower area. For Exercise 8, you would alternate the bass between the first beats of every measure.

When you are learning something new, it is best to concentrate on one thing at a time. If you are learning a new song, concentrate on learning the chord patterns. If you are learning a new rhythm technique, concentrate on a smooth and steady rhythm. Then, after those become comfortable, begin thinking about variations of tone and technique. Combinations of tones and techniques make music interesting and dynamic.

Beginning Strumming Techniques

Exercise 9a is the same rhythm as 9b only it is played in different areas of the strings. Compare the difference in sound.

EXERCISE 9

a.

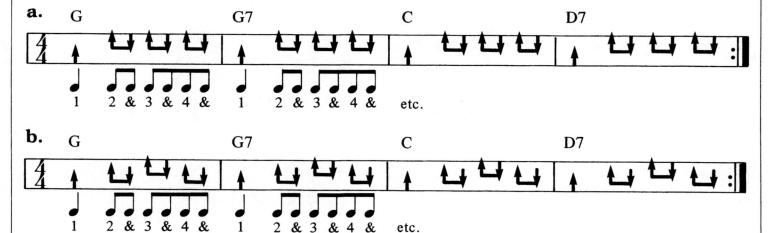

b.

Finger Positions

12-15 Bar Autoharp — Your middle finger rests on G, your index finger on C, your ring finger on D7, and your thumb is free to press the G7 chord bar.

21 Bar Autoharp — Center your thumb on G7, and your index finger on D7, and your ring finger plays both C and G.

Suggested Practice Songs

Down By the Riverside, page 36 (G)

When the Saints Go Marching In, page 40 (K)

EXERCISE 10

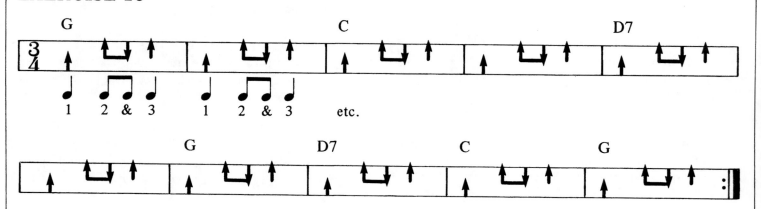

Finger Position

12-15 Bar Autoharp — Your middle finger centers on G, your index finger on C, and your ring finger on D7.

21 Bar Autoharp — Your thumb centers on C, your index finger on D7, and your ring finger on G.

Suggested Practice Songs

Daisy Bell, page 39 (J)

Greensleeves, page 42 (L)

Look at the first beat (1 &) of Exercise 11. The first strum is in the lower register strings, followed by a fingered strum in the higher strings.

EXERCISE 11

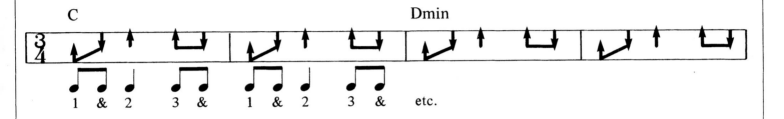

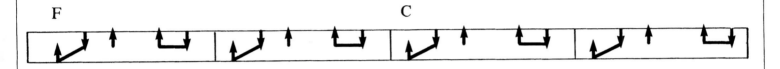

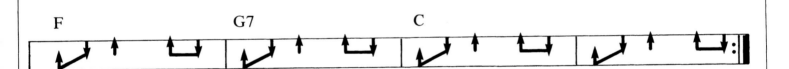

L.H. Finger Positions

12-15 Bar Autoharp — Your middle finger is centered on C, index finger on G7, and your thumb on F. Since the thumb is also needed to push the D minor chord bar, your finger positions will not remain the same throughout the chord progression, as follows: with your fingers centered, push the C chord with your middle finger (1st measure), then move your thumb back to the D minor (3rd measure). Your index finger will push the following F (5th measure) instead of your thumb. The next chord, C (7th measure), is pushed with the middle finger. Your fingers should return to the centered position to complete the rest of the chord progression, with the thumb pressing F (9th measure), the index finger pressing G7 (10th measure), and finally, the middle finger pressing C (11th measure).

For each song you choose to learn, you will develop a certain finger pattern. Your fingers will sometimes fall naturally into a pattern. Other times you will need to experiment to find the most comfortable and economical pattern. Always keep home base in mind. Once you have developed the finger pattern for a song, it usually remains the same each time you play it.

21 Bar Autoharp — Your ring finger is centered on C, your thumb on F, your index finger on G7, and your middle finger on D minor.

Suggested Practice Songs

Beautiful, Beautiful, Brown Eyes, page 37 (H)

Irene, Goodnight, page 43 (M)

Beginning Strumming Techniques

In the 7th measure of Exercise 12, there are two chord changes within one measure. You will find this happens in many songbooks.

EXERCISE 12

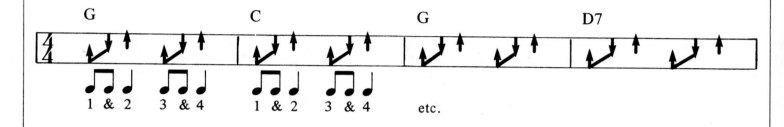

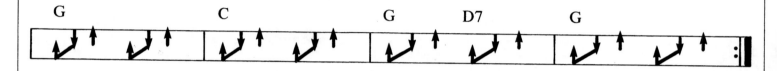

Finger Positions

12-15 Bar Autoharp — Your middle finger centers on G, your index finger on C, and your ring finger on D7.

21 Bar Autoharp — Your ring finger centers on G, your thumb on C, and your index finger on D7.

Suggested Practice Songs

Rock-A My Soul, page 38 (I)

Mama Don't 'Low, page 44 (N)

HINT: Try the alternating bass with this strum (see page 17).

Bonnie Phipps

When using the back and forth strumming motion as in Exercise 5, you can create different effects by strumming in the low area at different times. Exercise 13 gives some examples of this. These strums sound best when you put a large distance between your lower and higher strokes.

EXERCISE 13

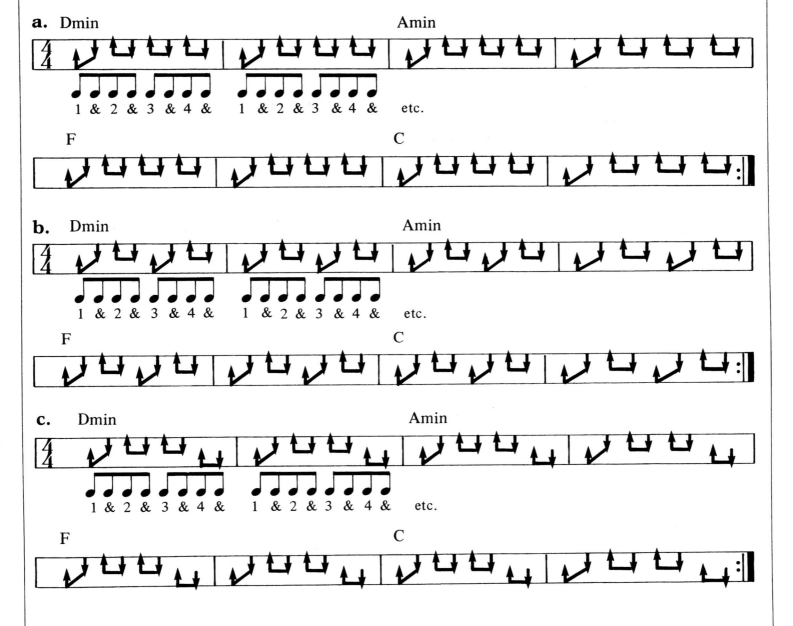

Finger Positions

12-15 Bar Autoharp — The thumb centers on D minor, the ring finger on A minor, the index finger on F, and the middle finger on C.

21 Bar Autoharp — The index finger centers on D minor, the middle finger on A minor, the thumb on F, and the ring finger on C.

Suggested Practice Songs

When the Saints Go Marching In, page 40 (K)

Drunken Sailor, Page 45 (O)

Beginning Strumming Techniques

Exercise 14a and b are other examples of different effects created by using different areas of the strings. If you clap out the rhythms, you will notice that they are the same. However, because of the placement of the low strum on the third count in Part b, a different effect is created.

EXERCISE 14

a.

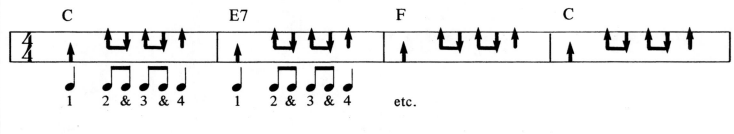

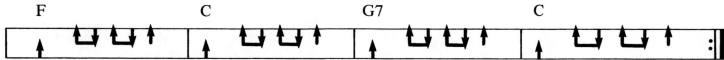

b. The alternating bass sounds great with this strum (see page 17).

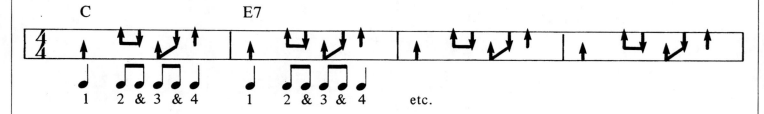

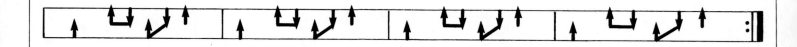

Finger Positions

12-15 Bar Autoharp — Your middle finger centers on C, your index finger on G7, your thumb on F, and your ring finger on E7.

21 Bar Autoharp — Your ring finger centers on C, your index finger on G7, and your thumb on F. Your middle finger is free to press E7.

Suggested Practice Songs

Mama Don't Low, page 44 (N)

Do Lord, page 47 (P)

Now you will learn a *syncopated* strum pattern. This means that there will be no strum on one (or more) of the downbeats, followed by a strum on an upbeat (see page 15 for an explanation of upbeats and downbeats). In Exercise 15, notice that there is an eighth note rest on the downbeat of the 3rd count. Therefore, you will only strike the strings on the upbeat of the 3rd count. Move your hand *as if* you were striking the strings with your thumb on the 3rd downbeat, but do not touch the strings. As you bring your fingers back for the upbeat, then strike the strings.

EXERCISE 15

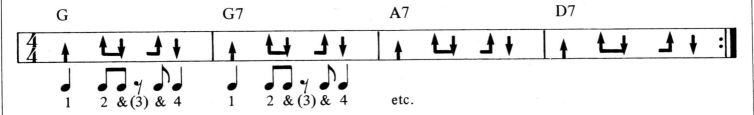

Finger Positions

12-15 Bar Autoharp — Your middle finger centers on G, your index finger on E7, your thumb on A7, and your ring finger on D7. This postion will take a little more coordination to remain centered. Try to keep your fingers in this position throughout the chord progression.

21 Bar Autoharp — Your ring finger centers on G, your middle finger on E7, your index finger on A7, and your thumb on D7.

Suggested Practice Songs

Mary Ann, page 29 (A)

Rock-A My Soul, page 38 (I)

THE PINCH

So far you have used your thumb and fingers alternately. Now, your thumb and one or more fingers will strike the strings at the same time in a pinching motion towards each other (Figure 12). This technique is called the *pinch* and is symbolized by two arrows coming together (⥮). The thumb covers an area of approximately 4-8 strings and the finger(s) covers an area of approximately 3-6 strings. Strike the strings in a light fashion but with enough force to produce a crisp tone. Keep your hand and fingers relaxed and as natural as possible.

Figure 12.

Beginning Strumming Techniques

Exercise 16 offers a few suggestions to help you become acquainted with the sounds you can produce with the pinch. You will use the pinch more in the chapter on Basic Melody. There is no *right* sound; try for sounds you like.

EXERCISE 16

• Press any chord(s) and practice pinching the strings at random, keeping a steady beat.

• Try a variety of distances between your thumb and finger(s) as you pinch. Each has a different effect. Begin with your thumb and finger(s) as far apart as possible, then try them closer together.

• Experiment with the number of fingers you use. Use one finger to play the high area as your thumb plays the low area. Use two fingers, one in the high area and one somewhat lower, as your thumb strikes the lowest strings. Use two fingers in the same area. Try three fingers, etc.

• Vary the number of strings your thumb and finger(s) strike. The song can range from delicate to full.

• Use different combinations of the low, middle, and high areas of the strings. Below are some examples. Use these pinching patterns to play some of the songs in Section B.

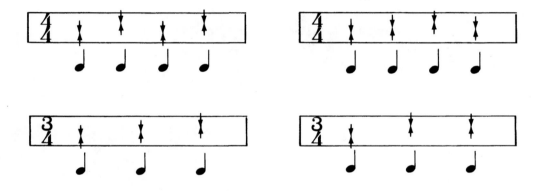

EXERCISE 17

Substitute the pinch for the thumb strokes (↑) that are in the low area of the strings in Exercises 7 through 15 (Figure 14).

Figure 14

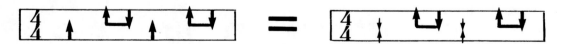

In doing this, you will discover that you are using your fingers in a way that you have never used them before. This exercise is important because it will aid you in alternating from melody-picking to strumming, and in fingerpicking later on. I find it helpful to pinch the strings with my thumb and middle finger (or middle and ring finger), and to play the finger strums (↓) with my index finger. This helps coordinate my fingers when I play a pinch immediately after a double strum (↑↓).

CHANGING CHORDS IN THE MIDDLE OF STRUM PATTERNS

When you use song-books you will notice that there are some chord changes in the middle of a measure. So far we have mainly used chord progressions that change at the beginning of a measure. In Exercises 18 through 22, you will use familiar techniques with more complicated chord changes. Study the exercises carefully to be sure you are making the chord changes at the correct time. The challenge is for the right hand to play the rhythm patterns continuously and that a chord change in the middle of it will not disturb the pattern. This may have to be worked out slowly at first.

Each exercise has two different rhythm patterns for the same chord progression. This will give you an idea of how you can create different effects by varying the strums. Part A is significantly easier than Part B. You may want to play all the A's first, and then all the B's, before you compare each set of exercises.

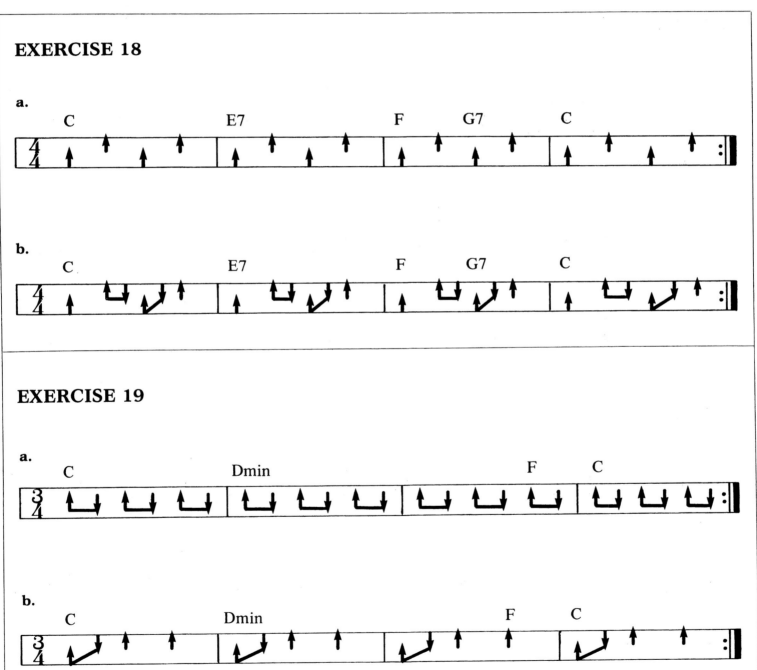

EXERCISE 18

a.

b.

EXERCISE 19

a.

b.

Beginning Strumming Techniques

EXERCISE 20

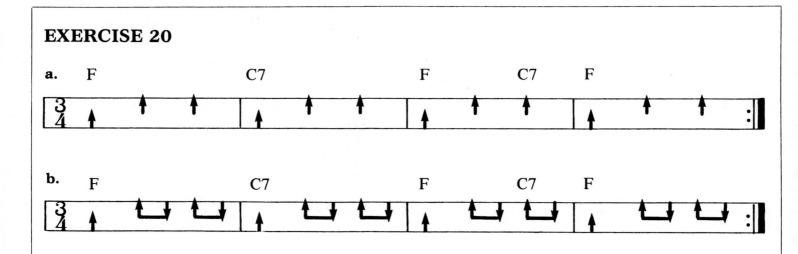

In Exercise 21, be aware of the difference between the 3rd measure and the first two. The first two measures have chord changes that occur on the first and third counts. The 3rd measure has chord changes that occur on the first and fourth counts.

EXERCISE 21

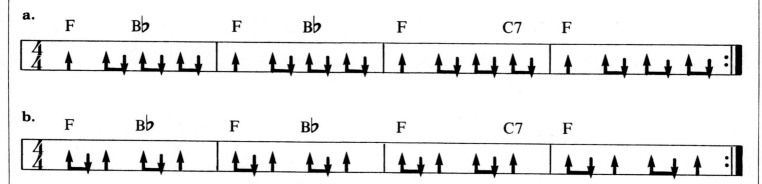

EXERCISE 22

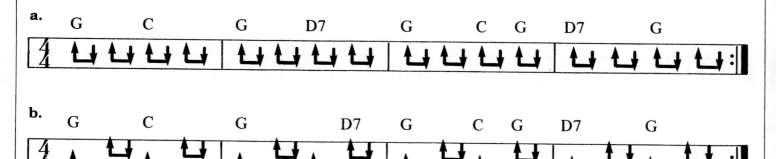

Suggested Practice Songs

In The Good Old Summertime, page 48 (Q)   Jamaica Farewell, page 49 (R)

COMBINING STRUM PATTERNS

An accompaniment becomes boring if you continuously use the same rhythm pattern. To make an accompaniment interesting, you need to change the strum pattern for different parts of a song. Exer-

cises 23 through 26 are examples of how you can combine the strum patterns you have learned. When you have finished these exercises, turn to Section B, pages 50–52, and there you will find the accompaniments written for the songs *House of the Rising Sun* and *Old Folks at Home*.

EXERCISE 23

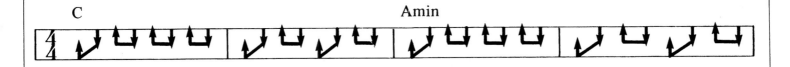

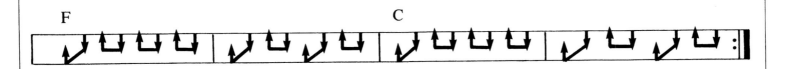

In the last measure of Exercise 24, there are two half-note strums. This means you are to strike the strings only on the 1st and 3rd beats.

EXERCISE 24

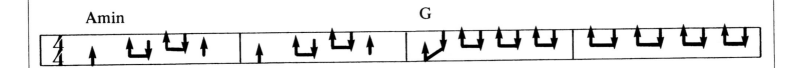

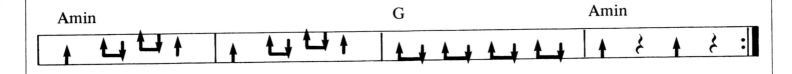

Beginning Strumming Techniques

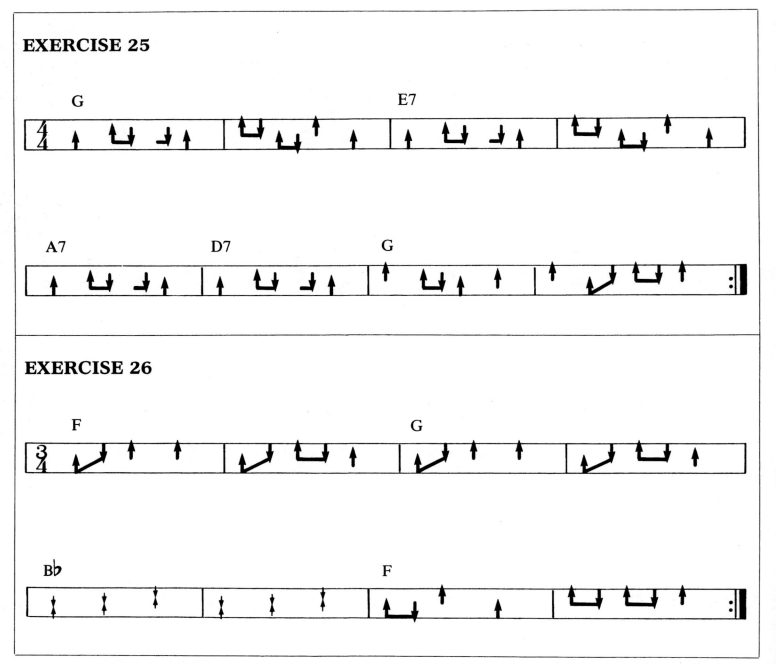

EXERCISE 25

EXERCISE 26

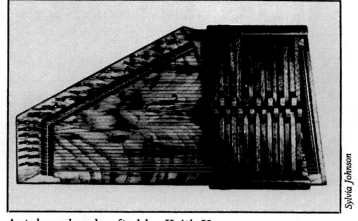

Autoharp handcrafted by Keith Young

Sylvia Johnson

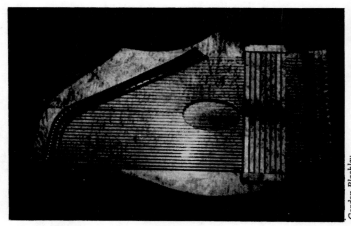

Autoharp made by Bob Welland

Gordon Blackley

SECTION B

SONGS

Strumming and singing involves a certain amount of coordination. You are doing two different things at the same time, strumming one rhythm pattern while singing another. You have already been playing the chords for *Mary Ann* in Exercise 1. Now you will learn to sing and play the song.

The slashes above the staff represent the beats in the measures. Use them as a guide for your strum patterns. The example below shows how the strum pattern from Exercise 1 fits with the beat. Notice, also, the relationship of the words to the beat. You can see that in the second measure you do not sing as you strum on the third and fourth beats.

It is important that you can hum the first few notes of a song before you begin playing and singing. The first note you sing in *Mary Ann* is an A note. You can tell because it is in the A space on the music staff (see Music Theory, page 75). Pluck the A note on the Autoharp and hum that note while you strum across the first chord in the song, which is F. Can you hear how the melody begins? If not, pluck the first two notes, etc.

MARY ANN

Chords: F, C7

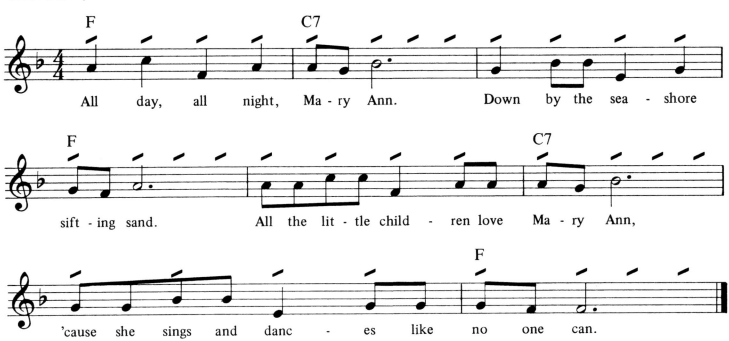

You begin strumming in the second measure (actually the first full measure) of *Buffalo Gals*. Get the first note (G) in your head. Now sing "As" and then begin strumming as you sing "I." Notice that in the chorus, the words you are singing are not always on the beat. See how the slashes (beats) fall between some of the words. Be careful to keep your strums on the beat as you sing the chorus.

BUFFALO GALS

Chords: C, G7

2. I danced with a gal with a hole in her stockin',
   And her heel kep' a-rockin' an' her toe kep' a-knockin'.
   I danced with a gal with a hole in her stockin',
   An' her heel kep' a-rockin' to the moon.

Begin singing *Clementine* on the third beat of the first measure. Begin strumming on the first beat of the second measure.

CLEMENTINE

Chords: C, G7

In a cav - ern, in a can - yon, ex - ca - vat - ing for a mine, dwelt a

min - er, for - ty nin - er, and his daugh - ter Clem - en - tine. Oh my

dar - ling, oh my dar - ling, oh my dar - ling Clem-en - tine, you are

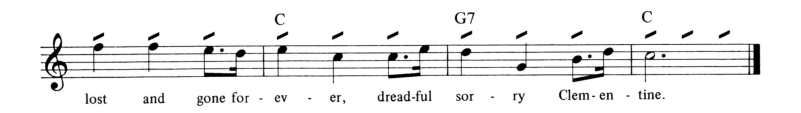

lost and gone for - ev - er, dread-ful sor - ry Clem-en - tine.

2. She drove ducklings to the water
   Every morning just at nine;
   Hit her big toe 'gainst a splinter,
   Fell into the foamin' brine.

3. Ruby lips above the water
   Blowing bubbles soft and fine;
   But alas! I was no swimmer,
   So I lost my Clementine.

Another way to find your first singing notes is to strum across the two or three main chords in the song and listen. Begin and end with the chord of the key the song is in. For example, if the song is in the key of C, play the C chord first. *Down In The Valley* is in the key of F. Strum across the F, C7, and then the F chord. Can you hear the first few notes you should sing as you return to the F chord? (See page 79, *Playing Simple Songs By Ear.*)

DOWN IN THE VALLEY

Chords: F, C7

2. Roses love sunshine, violets love dew;
   Angels in heaven know I love you.
   Know I love you, dear, know I love you,
   Angels in heaven know I love you.

Strum across the G, C, D7, then G chords to hear the beginning notes for *My Bonnie*.

MY BONNIE

Chords: G, C, D7

HINT: As you are first learning a song and developing finger positions,
use a very simple strum as in Exercise 1. Use a more complicated strum
when you have become familiar with the chord pattern of the song.

There are three places in *Oh Susanna* where there is a chord change in the middle of a measure. It may be difficult to play the strum pattern from Exercise 4 when this occurs. You can change that strum pattern for those particular measures as shown below:

(Notice that the strum pattern from Exercise 7 does not need to be changed for those measures.)

OH SUSANNA

Chords: F, C7, B♭

Now try strumming *before* you begin singing. In *Down By The Riverside*, begin your strum pattern at the beginning of the first measure as shown below. Begin singing on the fourth beat of that measure. This is called an *introduction*.

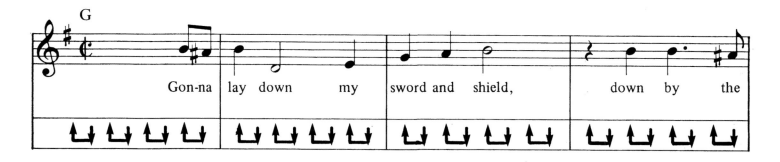

Gon-na lay down my sword and shield, down by the

Chuck Larsen

DOWN BY THE RIVERSIDE

Chords: G, C, D7

2. Gonna lay down my heavy load. . .
3. Gonna try on a starry crown. . . .
4. Gonna sit down and rest my soul. . . .

BEAUTIFUL, BEAUTIFUL BROWN EYES

Chords: G, C, D7

Wil - lie, oh Wil - lie, I love you,_____ love you with all my heart._____ To - mor - row we might have been mar - ried,_____ but lik - ker has kept us a - part._____

chorus

Beau - ti - ful, beau - ti - ful brown eyes,_____ beau - ti - ful, beau - ti - ful brown eyes,_____ beau - ti - ful, beau - ti - ful brown eyes,_____ I'll nev - er love blue eyes a - gain._____

2. Seven long years I've been married;
   I wish I was single again.
   A woman never knows of her troubles
   Until she has married a man.

3. Down to the bar room he staggered,
   Staggered and fell at the door.
   The last words that he ever uttered,
   "I'll never drink likker no more."

37

The following finger positions are suggested for *Rock-A My Soul* with the upright Autoharp:

12-15 Bar Autoharp — The middle finger rests on C, the index finger on G7, and the thumb presses both G minor and D minor.

21 Bar Autoharp — The ring finger rests on C, thumb on G7, index on G minor, and the middle finger on D minor.

ROCK-A MY SOUL

Chords: C, G7, Gm, Dm

DAISY BELL

Chords: F, B♭, C7, G7

Dai - sy, Dai - sy, give me your an - swer true._____ I'm half cra - zy,

all for the love of you._____ It won't be a styl - ish mar - riage,_____ I can't af - ford a car - riage._____ But you'll look

sweet up - on the seat of a bi - cy - cle built for two._____

2. Harry, Harry here is your answer true,
I'd be crazy if I ever married you.
If it won't be a stylish marriage
And you can't afford a carriage,
Then I'll be damned if I'll be crammed
On a bicycle built for two.

You can add an introduction to a song by strumming a few extra measures before you begin singing, even though it is not written in the music. Below is an example of how you can add a short introduction to *When The Saints Go Marching In*. You would begin singing on the second beat of the second measure you strum.

WHEN THE SAINTS GO MARCHING IN

Chords: C, F, G7, C7

2. And when the revelation comes . . . .
3. And when the sun refuse to shine . . . .
4. And when the new world is revealed . . . .
5. And when they gather 'round the throne . . . .
6. And on the hallelujah day . . . .

You can make up a short chord progression as an introduction for a song. Below is an example for *Greensleeves*:

Greensleeves has a fairly complicated chord progression. Below are suggested finger positions for the song. Sometimes it helps to pencil in the book a symbol by each chord indicating which finger is to press it.

12-15 Bar Autoharp — Your middle finger remains centered on C and your thumb on B♭. For the verse, the ring finger plays D minor and the index finger plays F and A7. For the second chorus of the song, the finger pattern goes as follows: Press the F (first measure of the chorus) with the index finger, the C (third measure) with the middle

finger, and the B♭ (fifth measure) with the thumb. You press the A7 (seventh measure) with the ring finger instead of the index finger because the index finger is needed to press the following F (ninth measure). Then press the C with the middle finger, B♭ with the thumb, the A7 with the index finger, and the D minor with the ring finger.

21 Bar Autoharp — Keep your ring finger centered on C and your middle finger on A7. Your index finger plays D minor and your thumb plays both B♭ and F.

Tom and Mary Morgan

John Rawlston, News-Free Press

GREENSLEEVES

Chords: Dm, C, B♭, F, A7

IRENE GOODNIGHT

Chords: G, G7, C, D7

The time signature for *Mama Don't 'Low* is 2/4. The strum patterns you will be using are in 4/4 but they can easily be adapted to a 2/4 rhythm as shown below.

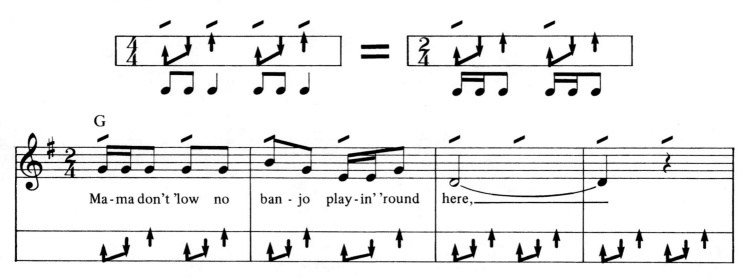

MAMA DON'T 'LOW

Chords: G, G7, D7, C

2. Mama don't 'low no slide trombones 'round here . . . .
3. Mama don't 'low no fancy singin' 'round here . . . .
4. Mama don't 'low no bass slappin' 'round here . . . .
5. Mama don't 'low no talk or chatter 'round here . . . .
6. Mama don't 'low no two-step dancin' 'round here . . . .

44

DRUNKEN SAILOR

Chords: Dm, Am, C

What shall we do with a drunk - en sail - or, what shall we do with a

drunk - en sail - or, what shall we do with a drunk - en sail - or,

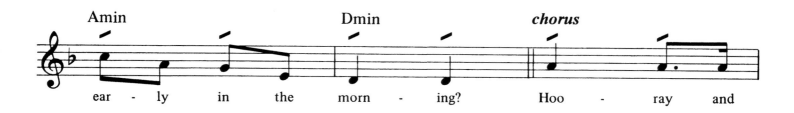

ear - ly in the morn - ing? Hoo - ray and

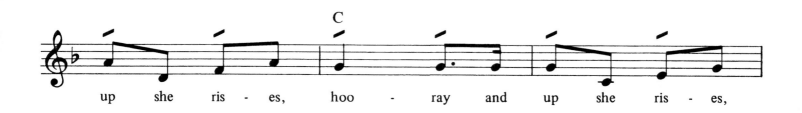

up she ris - es, hoo - ray and up she ris - es,

hoo - ray and up she ris - es, ear - ly in the morn - ing.

2. Put him in the longboat until he's sober . . . .
3. Scrape his belly with a rusty razor . . . .
4. Put him in the bilge and make him drink it . . . .
5. Keelhaul him until he's sober . . . .
6. Heave him by the leg in a running bowline . . . .

The time signature for *Do Lord* is 4/4. The time signature for the suggested strum pattern from Exercise 14 is also 4/4, yet they do not work well together unless you use two of that strum pattern for each measure. Here is how it can be done:

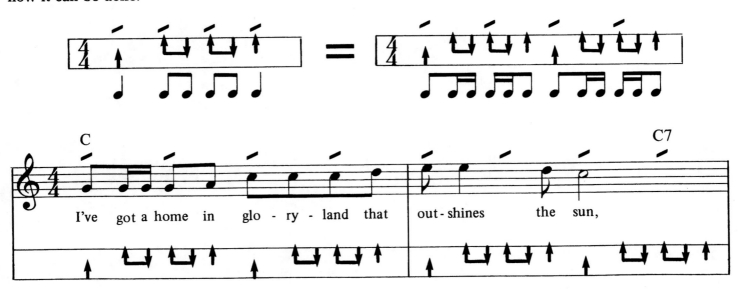

Try these finger positions for upright Autoharp for *Do Lord:*

12-15 Bar Autoharp — Your middle finger centers on C, your thumb on C7, and your ring finger on A minor. Keep your fingers in that position while the index finger plays F, G7, and E7.

21 Bar Autoharp — Your ring finger remains centered on C, and your thumb on C7. This is a difficult position to keep, as your middle finger plays E7 and your index finger plays the F, G7, and A minor chords. Try to keep at least your ring finger resting on C at all times. This will give you some basis from which to find the other chords.

Mike Seeger

John McCutcheon (Harp made by Robert Beers)

46

DO LORD

Chords: C, F, G7, C7, E7, Am

IN THE GOOD OLD SUMMERTIME

Chords: F, B♭, C7, G7, A7, Dm

Jamaica Farewell sounds especially nice with strum No. 15.

JAMAICA FAREWELL

Chords: F, Bb, C7, Am, Gm

1. Down the way where the nights are gay— and the sun shines dai-ly on the moun-tain top,— I took a trip on a sail-ing ship— and when I reached Ja-mai-ca I made a stop.— But I'm sad to say I'm on my way,— won't be back for man-y a day.— My heart is down— my head is turn-ing a-round,— I had to leave a lit-tle girl in Kings-ton-town. Kings-ton-town.

2. Sounds of laughter everywhere,
   And the dancing girls swaying to and fro.
   I must declare, my heart is there,
   Tho' I've been from Maine to Mexico.

3. Down at the market you can hear
   Ladies cry out while on their heads they bear
   Ack-ey rice, salt-fish are nice
   And the rum is fine anytime of year.

The last two songs are arranged to give you an idea of how to combine strum patterns in songs.

HOUSE OF THE RISING SUN

Chords: Am, Dm, F, C, D7, E7

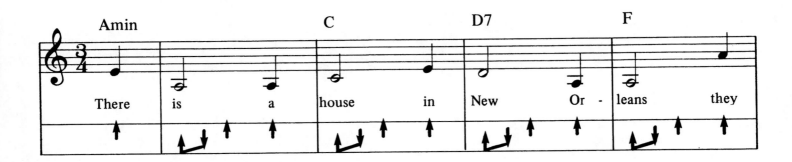

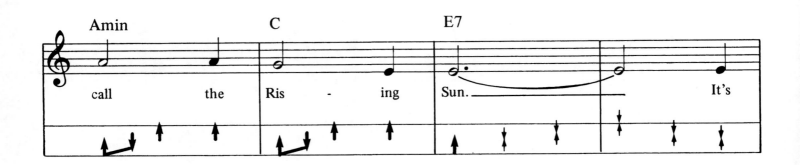

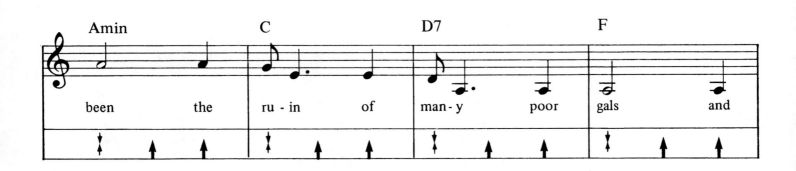

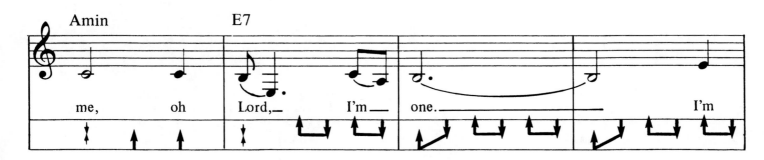

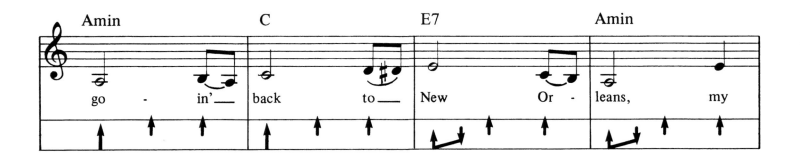

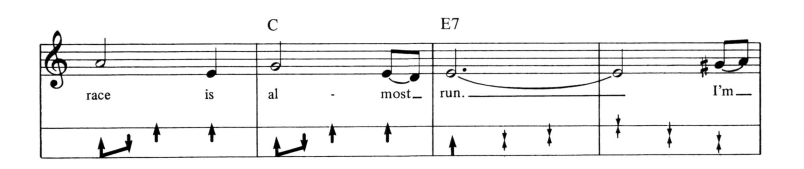

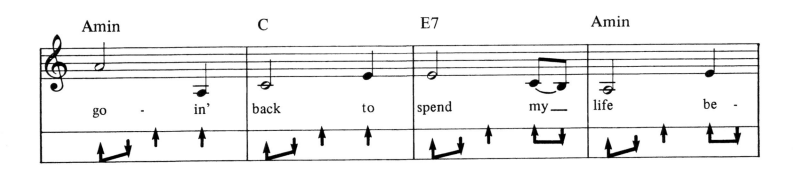

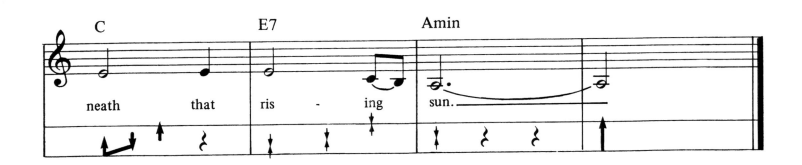

OLD FOLKS AT HOME

Chords: C, C7, F, G7

Stephen Foster

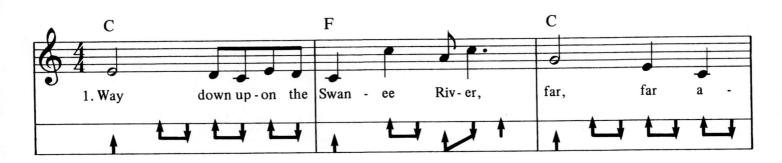

1. Way down up-on the Swan - ee Riv - er, far, far a -

way. There's where my heart is turn - ing ev - er,

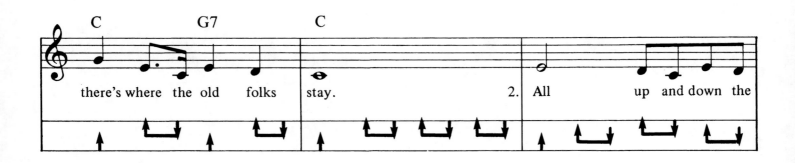

there's where the old folks stay. 2. All up and down the

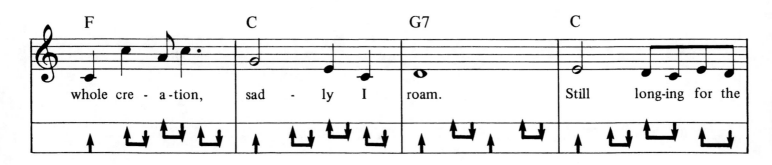

whole cre - a -tion, sad - ly I roam. Still long-ing for the

old plan - ta -tion   and for the old folks at home.

chorus

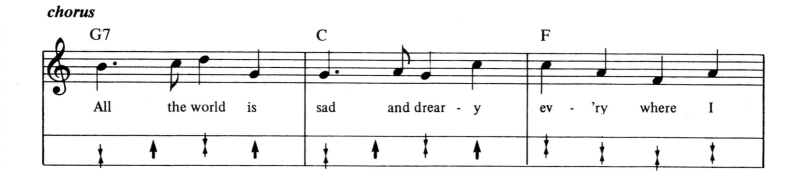

All   the world is   sad   and drear - y   ev - 'ry   where I

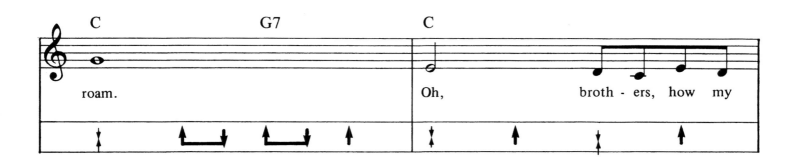

roam.   Oh,   broth - ers, how my

heart grows wea-ry,   far from the old   folks at home.

Beginning Strumming Techniques

Michael Stanwood

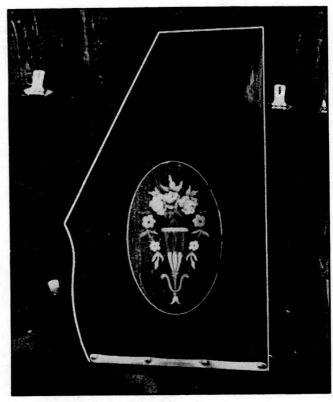

Autoharp made by Tom Morgan

Andy Boarman

David Holt

III. Basic Melody Techniques

In this chapter you are going to learn to play melody with the pinch technique discussed on page 23. But now, one finger will specifically sound the melody notes as your thumb sounds any lower notes. Most Autoharp players use their middle finger. The dampening effect of the chord bars allows you to strike the strings in the general vicinity of the melody note and still produce the note. It is important that you do not sound any notes that are higher in pitch than the melody note, as this confuses the melody. Lower notes are O.K. Harmonies can be produced by pinching the strings with several fingers spread apart. However, it is best to use your thumb and only one finger at first. The melody notes should sound louder than the other notes. This is done by striking the melody notes harder. Try for a bright, crisp tone.

As you play melody, you will make chord-changes more often than when you play accompaniments. This is because the melody notes are not always found in the chords used for the accompaniment. Those notes that are not in the accompaniment chord are called *passing notes*. You will need to push a different chord bar to sound those notes. In this chapter, the chord-changes for the

melody are written under each word, and the chord-changes for the accompaniment are written above the staff.

Kilby Snow, an "old timey" Autoharp player and innovator*, said that you cannot play a tune on the Autoharp unless you have it clearly in your head. Then, as you become familiar with the instrument, your ear will guide your fingers toward the correct strings. That may sound unbelievable, but it is true! As you hear the melody progress higher in pitch, your right hand will automatically move towards the higher strings. As it goes lower, your hand will move accordingly. In time, you will feel the relationship between how far you will have to move your fingers from one note to another.

If you are having trouble finding the notes by ear use the string indicator on this page. Cut it out and tape it to the side of the chord bar nearest you as you play in the upright position (Figure 13a). If you play with the Autoharp on your lap, place the string indicator beneath the strings (Figure 13b). Align the numbers with the strings, beginning with the lowest string (F) as number 1, and the highest string (C) as number 36. The correct string number for each note will be written above the words. Eventually you will want to learn to depend less and less on the string indicator and let your ear guide your hand.

Begin by playing the C and G scales on page 56. A chord accompanies each note of the scale. First strum across each chord and listen for the melody notes. Then use the pinch technique to play the notes in the scales. You need only to move your fingers slightly from one note to the next. Get the notes in your head and remain on each chord until you have found the correct note.

*See Discography for a list of recordings.

Figure 13a.

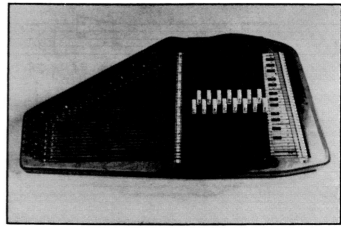

Figure 13b.

Basic Melody Techniques

Scale of C

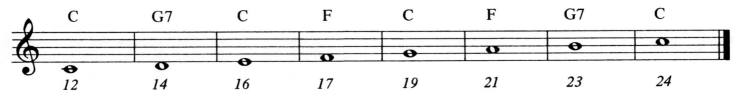

Scale of G

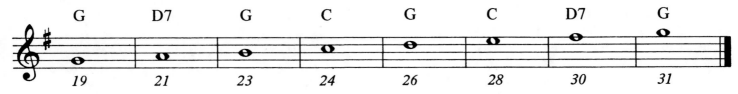

Can you figure out the scale of F by ear? Use the chords F, C7, Bb (see the Theory Section *Playing Songs By Ear*).

HINT: If you are having trouble hitting the correct notes, try using only one finger to play the note; then use the pinch.

Taps uses only one chord, C. Strum across the chord and hum the tune to yourself before playing it. Compare the movement of your fingers from note to note when you play *Taps* to when you play scales. As in the chapter on *Strumming Techniques,* the symbols will be tied together when they occur within the same beat.

TAPS

In the song *Ten Little Indians* the melody notes stay mainly within the accompaniment chords except in the second to the last measure.

TEN LITTLE INDIANS

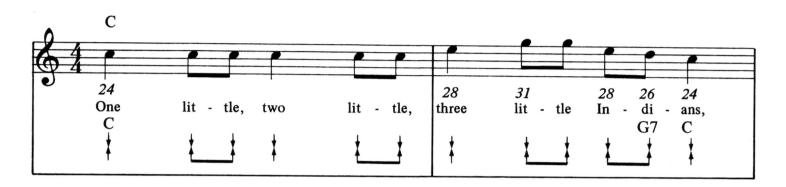

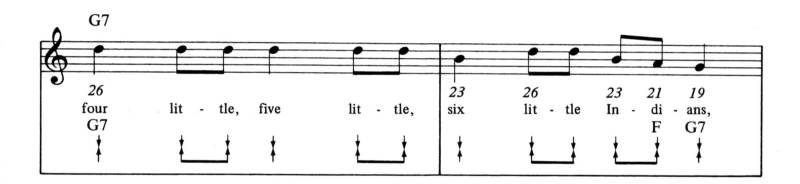

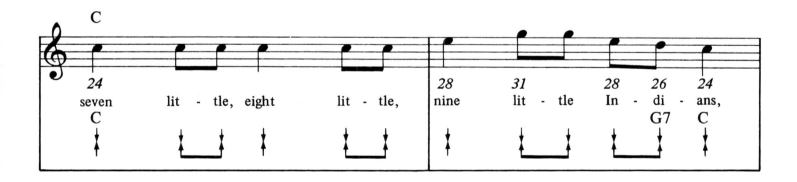

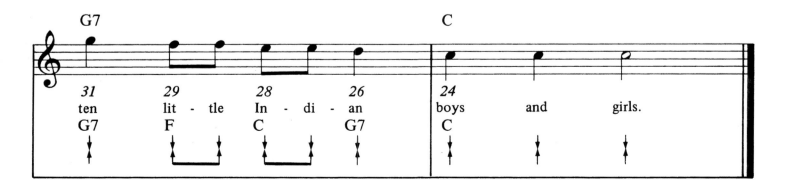

When there are pauses between the melody notes, you will want to fill them in with various strumming patterns. The next song, *Skip to My Lou*, has a few places where a strum would be appropriate. The symbols from the chapter on *Strumming Techniques* are suggested ways to fill in the pauses. It will not be indicated in this chapter in which areas of the strings you are to strum. That will be up to you.

In some measures, the count is written beneath the tablature. This is to help you read the correct rhythm of the symbols when something new is introduced. In the 2nd measure of *Skip to My Lou* you can see that a strum occurs on the 4th beat.

SKIP TO MY LOU

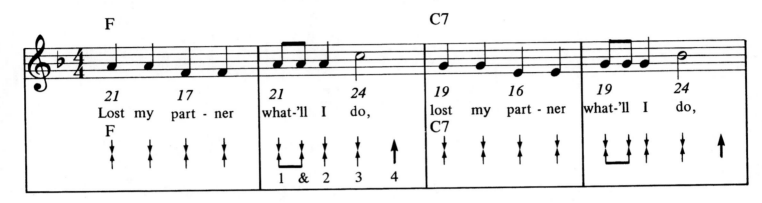

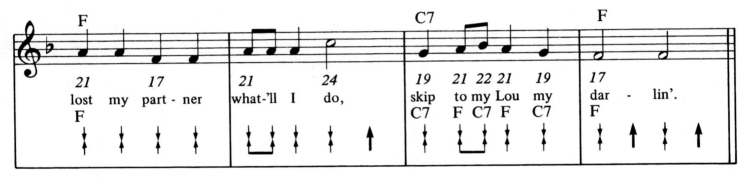

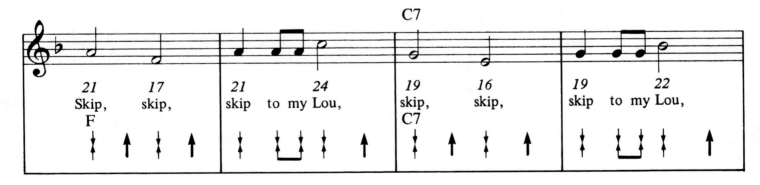

Usually a strum is appropriate when there is no note played on a downbeat. For example, in the 4th measure of *Clementine* the first note is held half-way through the 2nd beat so we will add a strum on that 2nd beat.

CLEMENTINE

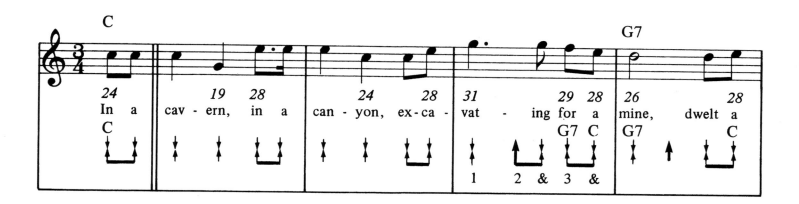

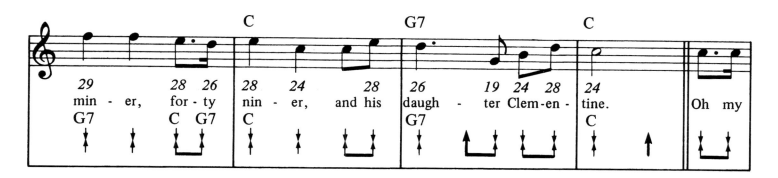

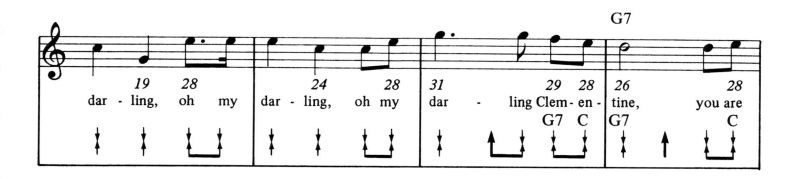

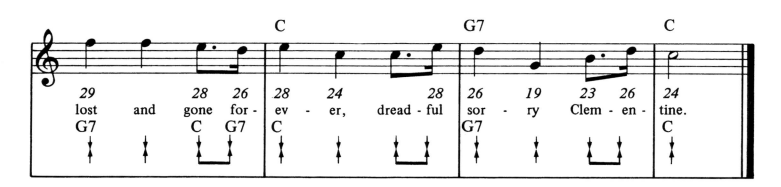

LULLABY

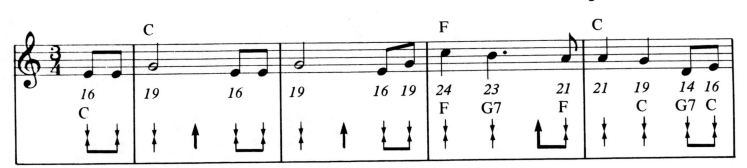

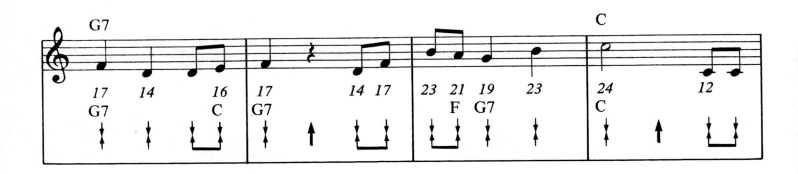

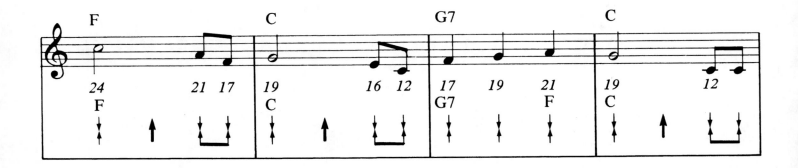

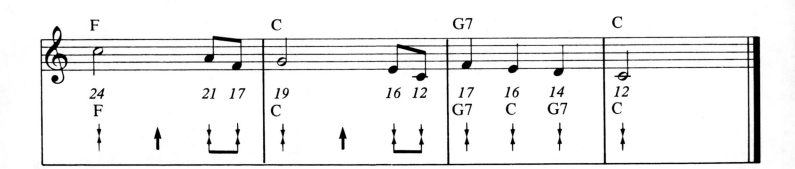

HINT: Are you having trouble accurately pinching from one note to another in certain places of a song? Try taking that section and practicing it a number of times until you get the feel of how your hand (and arm) needs to move from one note to the next.

BLUE DANUBE WALTZ

Johann Strauss

Now try some fill-in strums that are a bit more complicated. The following tunes will use combinations of the strums that you have already learned. *Irene Goodnight* uses one fill-in strum that is similar to the strum in Exercise 10, page 18. *When The Saints Go Marching In* uses one similar to Exercise 9, page 18.

IRENE GOODNIGHT

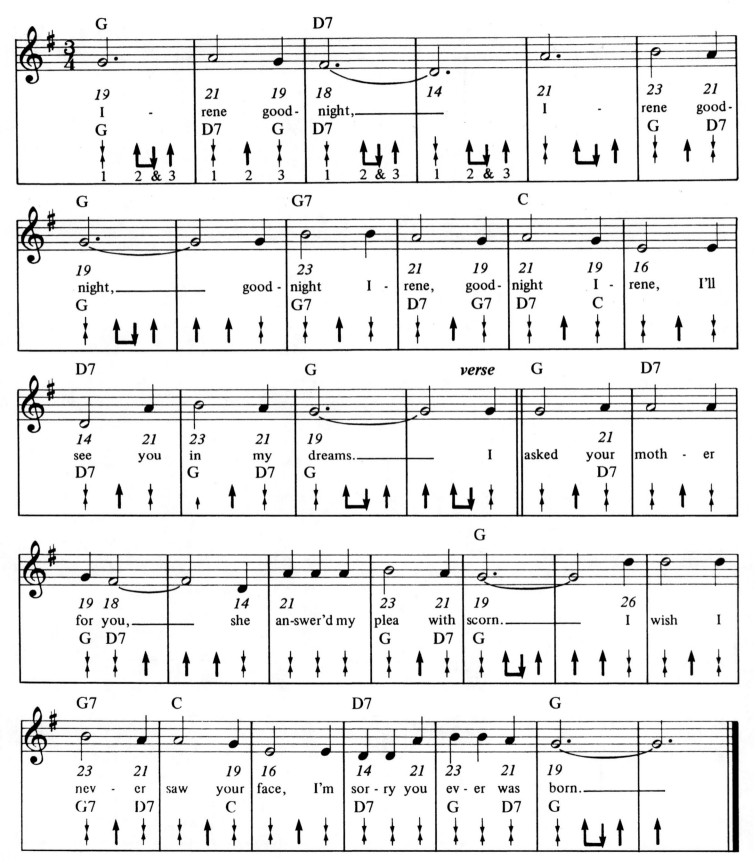

WHEN THE SAINTS GO MARCHING IN

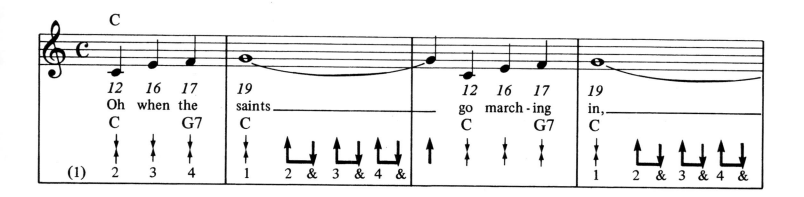

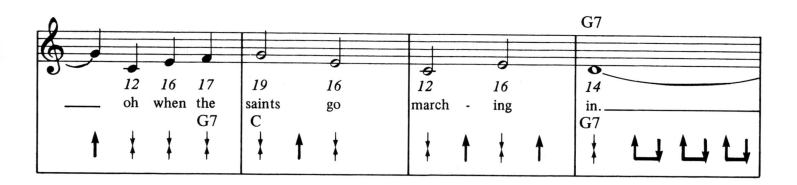

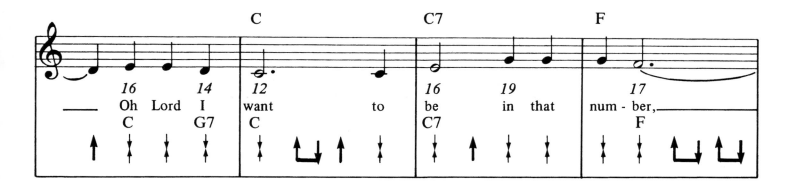

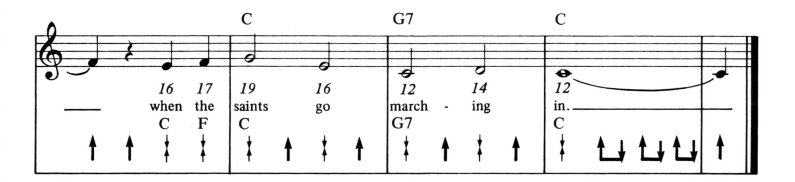

HINT: Are the strums confusing you as you are learning the melodies? If so, learn to play the melodies first, then add the strums.

RED RIVER VALLEY

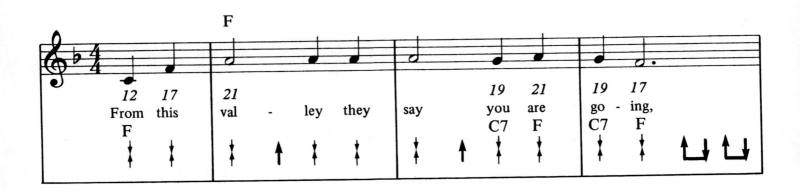

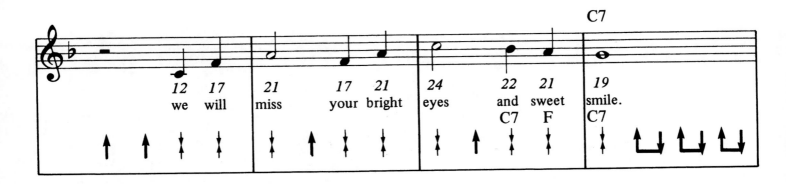

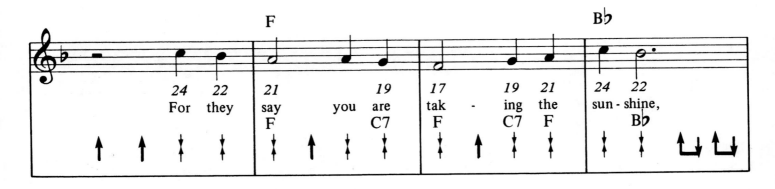

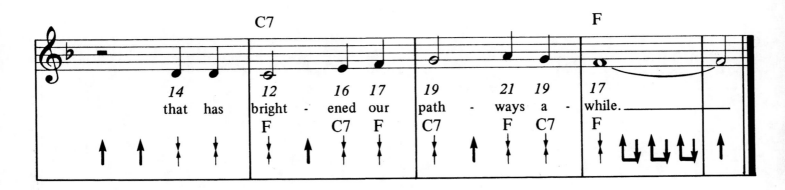

HINT: Try playing *Red River Valley* in the lower register. You will have to use your ear to tell you where to go since you are given the string numbers for only the higher register. Try this with other songs.

DAISY BELL

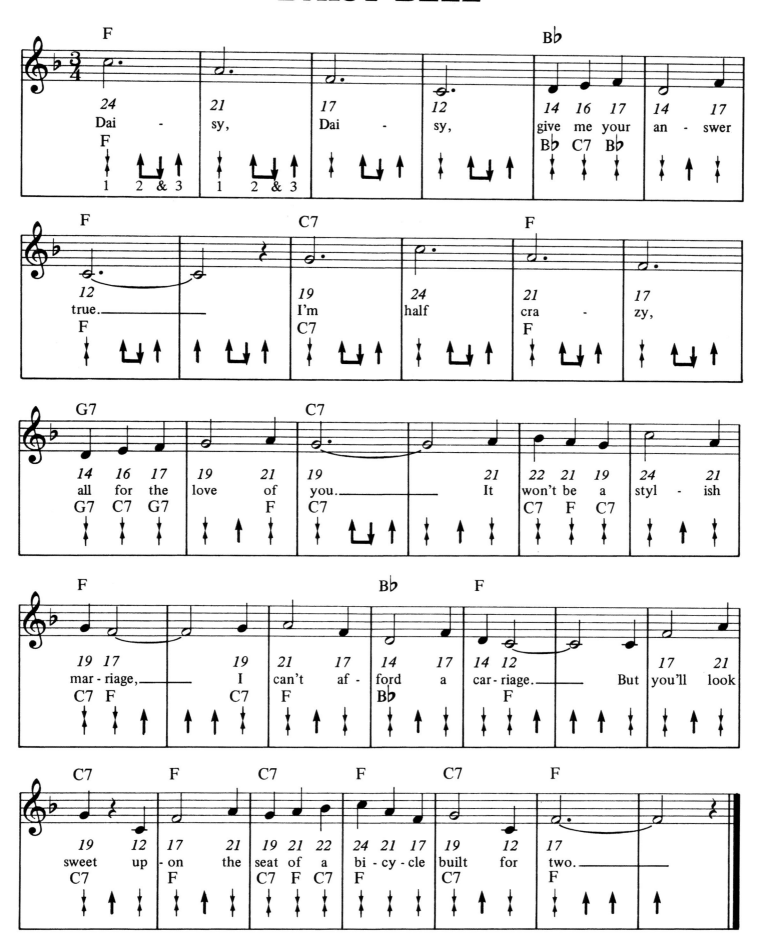

BATTLE HYMN OF THE REPUBLIC

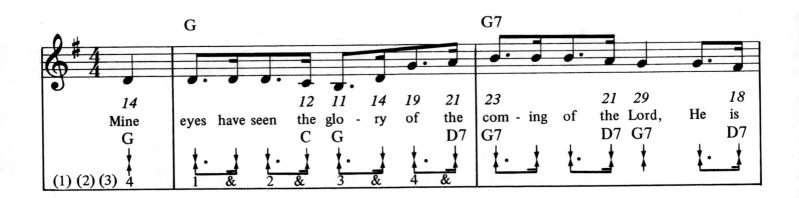

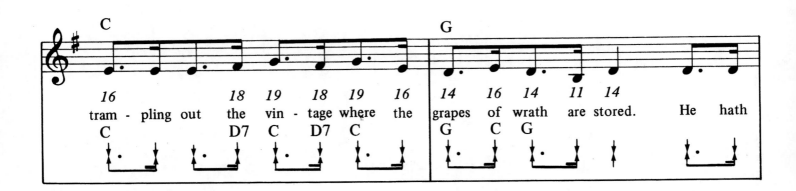

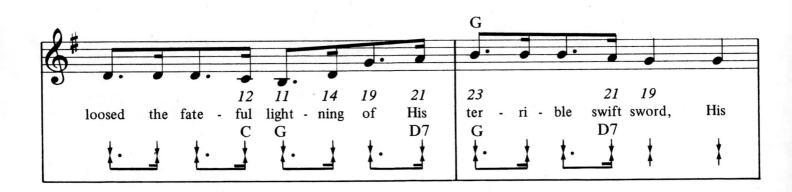

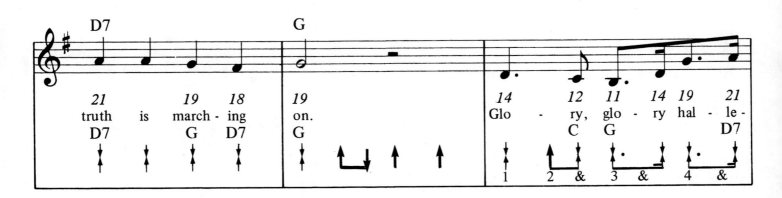

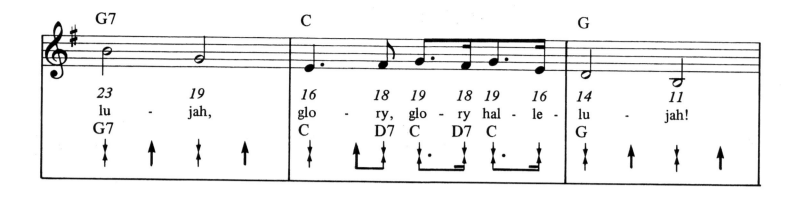

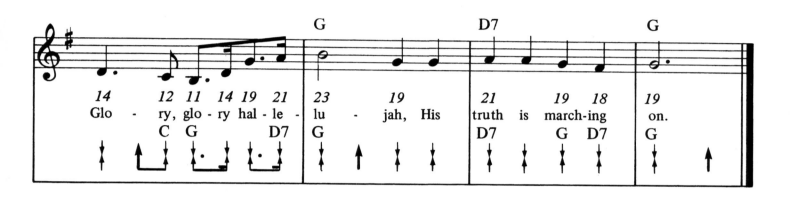

"Sweet Betsy from Pike" Autoharp Band

SIMPLE GIFTS

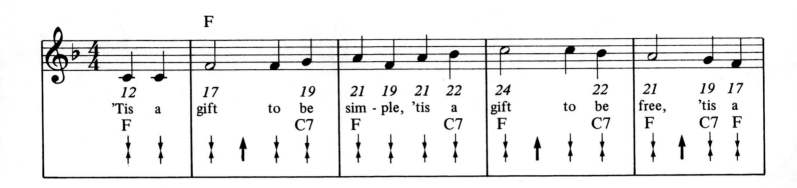

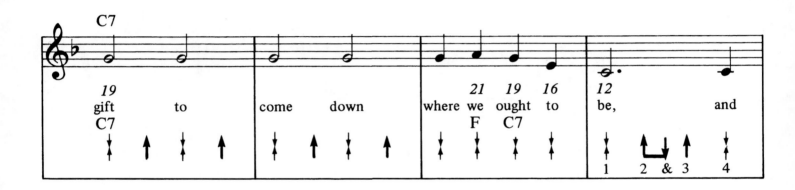

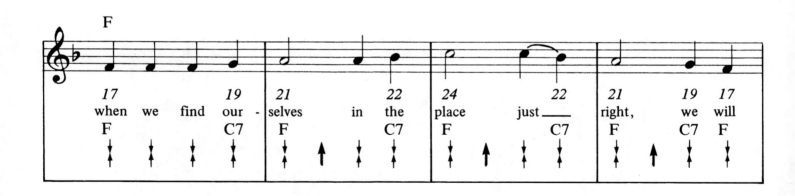

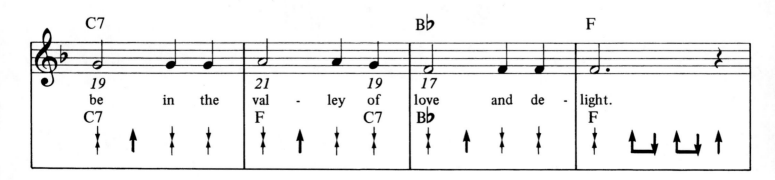

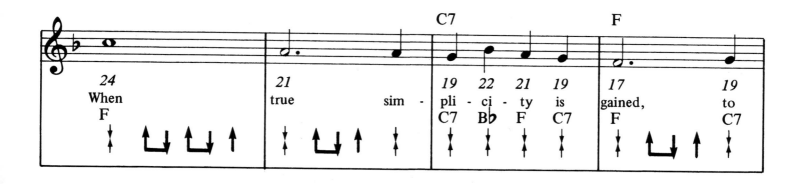

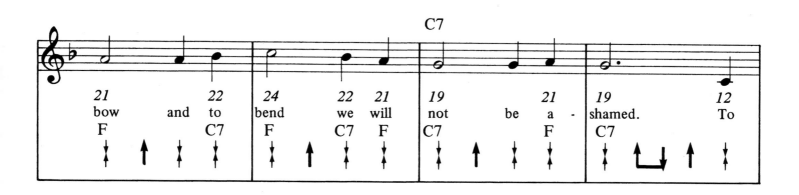

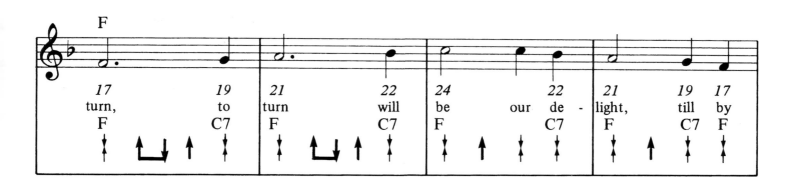

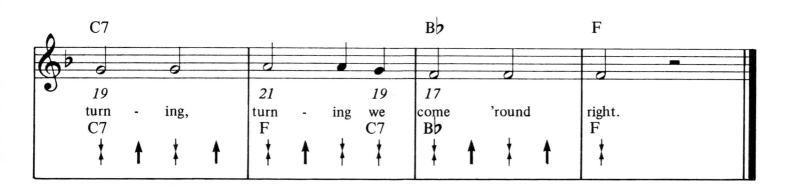

You do not always have to play a melody exactly as it is written. Sometimes it is easier or desirable to leave out certain notes. For example, if the same note is played a number of times in rapid succession, it may sound better on the Autoharp to play only a few of those notes. Or if a portion of a melody line is rhythmically hard to play, you may want to play only the key notes in that section. Learn the songs *She'll Be Comin' 'Round the Mountain* and *Old Molly Hare* as an introduction to leaving out notes.

In *She'll Be Comin' 'Round the Mountain* some of the melody notes are syncopated and may be hard to play, so these notes will not be played. The *pinches* (↕) are written only under the notes that are to be sounded. For example, in the 2nd measure you play only the notes that occur on the 1st and 3rd beats and fill in the 2nd and 4th beats with a strum.

SHE'LL BE COMIN'
'ROUND THE MOUNTAIN

In *Old Molly Hare* you are leaving out quite a few notes to avoid sounding tedious. Basically, you are playing the skeleton of the song. A similar version of this song can be heard on the *Mountain Music Played on The Autoharp* album (see Discography).

OLD MOLLY HARE

Now that you know how you can simplify a song, here is a way to play some tunes that are more rhythmically complicated. If you tap your foot and sing a song, some of the notes will fall on the tap (on the *down-beat*) and some will fall between the taps (on the *off-beat*). The notes that fall on the off-beat are called *syncopated* notes. When a note occurs on an off-beat, you can use just one finger — for example, your index or middle finger — to play the note instead of a pinch. This means that sometimes your finger will be working faster than your thumb. This technique makes it easier to play syncopated melodies. Learn the song *Home On The Range* and *Rock-A My Soul* as an introduction to playing syncopated melodies. The symbol **O** will be used to indicate when only one finger is used to play a note.

In *Home On The Range* notice that some of the **O**'s follow pinches (as in the 3rd measure, 3rd beat) and some follow a strum and occur just before a pinch (as in the 14th measure, 2nd beat). This will require some additional coordination. You may find it helpful to alternate your middle and index finger; try pinching with the thumb and middle finger and playing the **O**'s with the index finger. However, this is not necessarily easier for everyone.

HOME ON THE RANGE

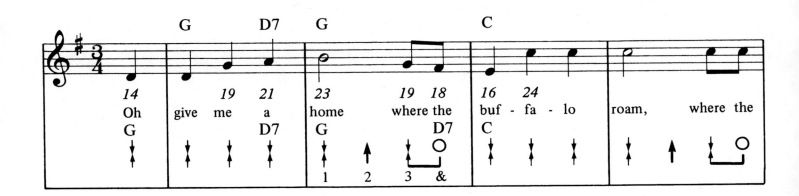

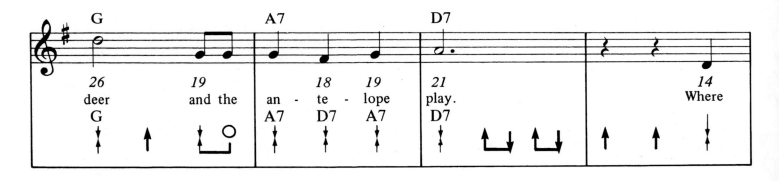

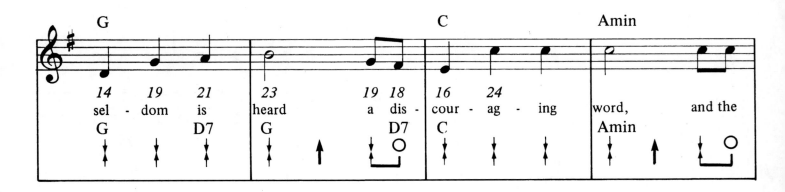

72

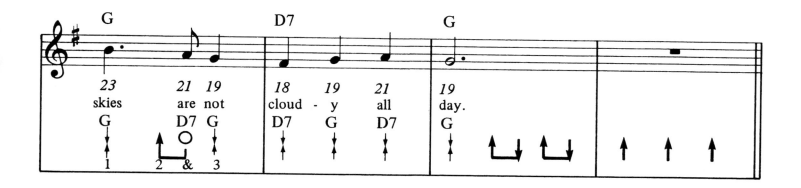
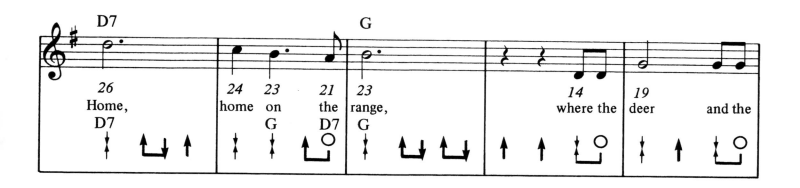
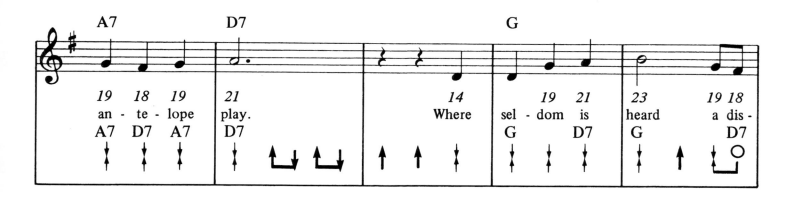
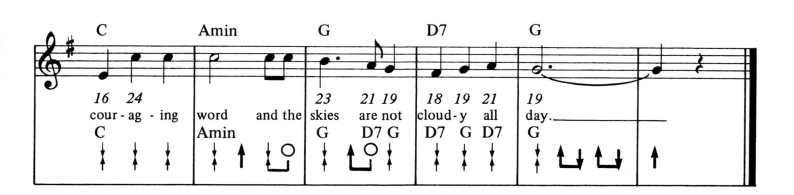

It is "sink-or-swim" with *Rock-A My Soul* — this is a very syncopated song. Good Luck!

ROCK-A MY SOUL

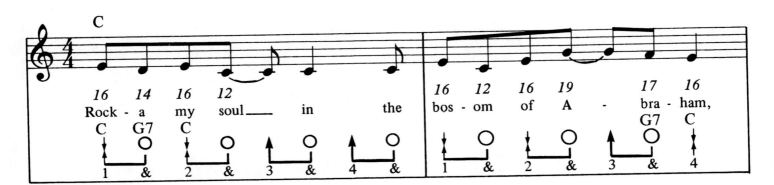

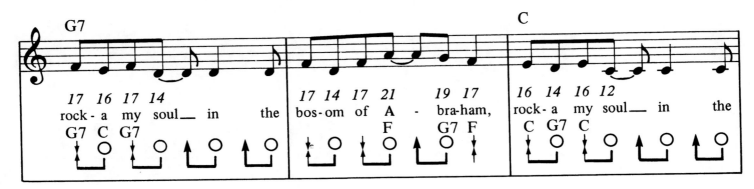

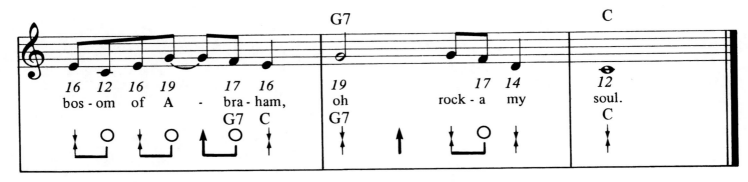

Bryan Bowers

John McCutcheon (autoharp) with another member of "Wry Straw"

Appendix A:
Basic Music Theory

KEY SIGNATURES

At the beginning of a song you will often see the symbols ♯ for sharps and ♭ for flats written next to the clef sign on the staff. A sharp means ½ step higher; a flat means ½ step lower. Autoharp strings are tuned in ½ steps (except at the very bottom). Look at a D note in the middle of your Autoharp. One fret higher is a D♯ and one fret lower is a C♯, which is the exact same note as a D♭.

Whenever sharps or flats appear on the staff at the beginning of a song, that means to raise or lower *all* those notes in the song ½ step. For example, if there are 2 sharps (F & C) in the key signature, ![key signature] then *all* the F and C notes in the song are F♯ and C♯.

THE GRAND STAFF

Musical notes appear on a series of five horizontal lines called a *staff*. Each line and the spaces between are assigned a letter. Seven letters are used: A B C D E F G. These letters correspond to the notes or pitches used in our music notation system. Each staff begins with a *clef* sign. There are two clef signs: a treble clef (𝄞) and a bass clef (𝄢). Each clef sign indicates which letters are assigned to the lines and spaces in the staff (see Figure A). The bass clef houses the lower notes and the treble clef houses the higher notes. Sometimes extra lines (called *leger lines*) are added below or above a staff. These are for notes that are higher or lower than those on the staff. In this book, you will use only the treble clef.

NOTE & REST VALUES

Each note is given a time value which indicates the duration of a note's musical sound. The time value of each note is measured in steady beats or counts. The relative time value of the notes that will be used in this book is shown on the next page in Figure B.

If you were playing a whole note, you would hold that note for four counts before playing the next one. If you were playing a half note, you would hold it for two counts before going on, and so on. Notice that you can play four quarter notes in the same amount of time as it takes to play one whole note. You can play two eighth notes in the same time as one quarter note. How many eighth notes can you play in the same amount of time as one half note?

Figure A:

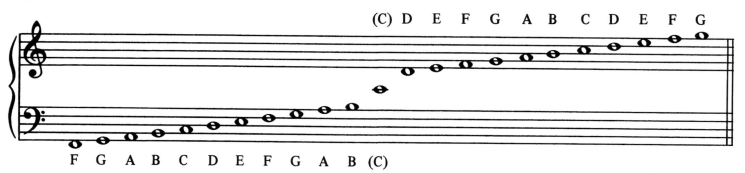

Figure B:

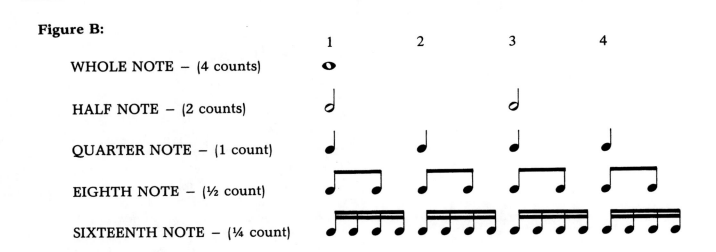

	1	2	3	4
WHOLE NOTE – (4 counts)	𝅝			
HALF NOTE – (2 counts)	𝅗𝅥		𝅗𝅥	
QUARTER NOTE – (1 count)	♩	♩	♩	♩
EIGHTH NOTE – (½ count)	♫	♫	♫	♫
SIXTEENTH NOTE – (¼ count)	♬♬	♬♬	♬♬	♬♬

Eighth notes and sixteenth notes can be linked together by their flags. Two eighth notes linked together would look like this ♫ . Two sixteenth notes would look like this ♬ . A dotted note (♩.) means that you add half of its time value to the note. A dotted half note would be equal to a half note plus a quarter note. It would be held for 3 counts.

A rest symbolizes silence. Rests are also given time values as shown in Figure C below.

Figure C:

	1	2	3	4
WHOLE REST – (4 counts)	▬			
HALF REST – (2 counts)	▬		▬	
QUARTER REST – (1 count)	𝄽	𝄽	𝄽	𝄽
EIGHTH REST – (½ count)	𝄾 𝄾	𝄾 𝄾	𝄾 𝄾	𝄾 𝄾
SIXTEENTH REST – (¼ count)	𝄿 𝄿 𝄿 𝄿	𝄿 𝄿 𝄿 𝄿	𝄿 𝄿 𝄿 𝄿	𝄿 𝄿 𝄿 𝄿

TIME SIGNATURES

Each staff is divided into portions by vertical lines called *bar lines*. The portions between the bar lines are called *measures*. The symbol that indicates the time value of each measure is called the *time signature*. It is written in the form of a fraction and is found at the beginning of each musical piece next to the clef (Figure D).

The top number tells how many counts each measure gets. The bottom number shows which type of note gets one count. In this book (and in many song-books), the bottom number will usually be 4. This means that a quarter note will get one count. In Figure D, the top number is 4 so there will be four counts to each measure. Notice that the time value of the notes in each measure always adds up to four counts. When the top number is 3, there will be three counts to each measure, and the notes in each measure will add up to three counts, and so on. Notice how the measures use different combinations of notes to make up their allotted counts.

Figure D:

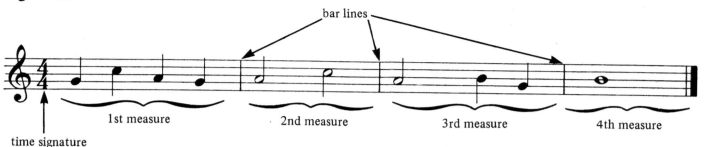

It is important to develop a *feel* for moving from one measure to the next. When you tap your foot to music, you are tapping a steady beat. Various rhythms occur on and around the beat but the beat is always there, like the ticking of a clock. The first beat of each measure is usually accented by playing it a bit louder. In 4/4 time the feel would be ONE, two, three, four, ONE, two, three, four, as in a march. In 3/4 time it would be ONE, two, three, ONE, two, three, as in a waltz. The symbol for an accent is >.

"Hoofin' High Country Cloggers," Denver, Colorado

Basic Music Theory

CLAPPING EXERCISES

To help you play the exercises in this book, it will be useful to learn to clap out the rhythms of the notes and, at the same time, feel the steady beat of each measure. At first, you will need to count mentally while you are playing until you begin to feel the beat naturally. Figure E is a series of exercises that help you to count out the steady beat of each measure while clapping out the rhythms of the notes. It is a good idea to clap out the rhythm of the exercises in this book before you play them. Clap once for each note — it will help you hear what the rhythms are supposed to sound like.

In the first exercise, you clap only once on the 1st count of the first measure and count to 4. In the second measure, you clap twice, once on the 1st count, and again on the 3rd count. In the third measure, you clap on every beat. In the fourth measure, you clap twice for every beat; the verbal count would be 1 and 2 and 3 and 4 and. Try keeping a steady beat with your foot while you clap out the rhythms. Have a friend who knows about music check to see if you are doing the exercises right.

Figure E:

TRANSPOSING

Many of the songs you will learn will be from songbooks. Since the Autoharp has a limited number of keys available, it is important that you know how to *transpose* from one key to another. There are many methods of transposing. I am going to show you how to use the chord chart below (Figure F). The chart shows the most common major keys and their basic chords.

Let's transpose the song *Pop Goes The Weasel* (page 81). You will transpose it to the key of F. First you need to determine what key the song is written in. The key signature is found at the beginning of the staff between the clef and the time signature. It is written in the form of sharps (♯) or flats (♭). For your reference, Figure G (page 80) lists the most basic keys and their key signatures. You can also tell by checking the first and last chord of the song. Songs often begin and end with the chord of the key

it was written in. For example, *Pop Goes The Weasel* begins and ends with a C chord, so it is in the key of C. It also has no sharps or flats.

Study Figure F. Now look at the first chord in *Pop Goes the Weasel* — it is a C chord. Note that in the key of C, a C chord is a I chord. Find the I chord in the key of F — it is F. Change all the C chords to F chords. (You can write the changes in pencil above the regular chords.) Now let's transpose the G chord. The chord chart shows that it is the V chord in the key of C. The V chord in the key of F is C, so all the G's will be changed to C's. Next you will transpose the D minor, a ii chord in the key of C. The ii chord in the key of F is G minor; change the D minors to G minors. The G7 chord is the V7 chord in the key of C; what would it be in the key of F? What will you change the A minor and the F major to?*

*Change the G7 to C7, the A minor to D minor, and the F major to B♭ major.

Figure F:

CHORD CHART

CHORDS:	I	ii	iii	IV	V	vi	vii°
MAJOR KEY							
C	C maj.	D min.	E min.	F maj.	G maj.	A min.	B°
D	D maj.	E min.	F♯ min.	G maj.	A maj.	B min.	C♯°
E	E maj.	F♯ min.	G♯ min.	A maj.	B maj.	C♯ min.	D♯°
F	F maj.	G min.	A min.	B♭ maj.	C maj.	D min.	E°
G	G maj.	A min.	B min.	C maj.	D maj.	E min.	F♯°
A	A maj.	B min.	C♯ min.	D maj.	E maj.	F♯ min.	G♯°
B	B maj.	C♯ min.	D♯ min.	E maj.	F♯ maj.	G♯ min.	A♯°
B	B♭ maj.	C min.	D min.	E♭ maj.	F maj.	G min.	A°

There are seven notes in a key. Each of those notes has a chord built upon it. The chords are numbered from 1 (beginning with the note of the key) to 7 in Roman numerals. Notice that the first, fourth, and fifth chords (I, IV, V) are major (maj.) chords. Major chords have a specific type of sound. The second, third, and sixth chords (ii, iii, vi) are minor (min.). Minor chords also have a distinctive sound as do all other types of chords. The seventh chord (vii°) in a

key is called a diminished chord and is used infrequently. The V chord in a key is often used as a V7 chord. This means that an extra note is added to the chord. In many songs, the V7 chord is used in place of the V chord. In the key of C, the V7 chord would be G7; in the key of F, it would be C7. What would it be in the key of G?*

*D7

Figure G:

KEY	SIGNATURE	KEY	SIGNATURE

No sharps or flats

C

One sharp

G

Two sharps

D

Three sharps

A

Four sharps

E

Five sharps

B

One flat

F

Two flats

B♭

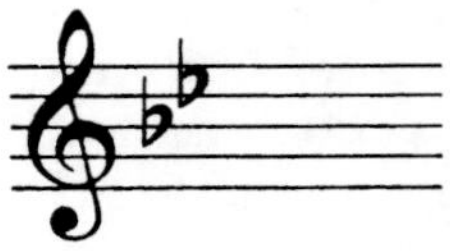

POP GOES THE WEASEL

You can use the chord chart to transpose most songs. One word of caution. Sometimes a ii, iii, or vi chord may be a major chord instead of a minor chord. If that happens, you simply transpose that chord to a major chord also.

PLAYING SIMPLE SONGS BY EAR

The trick to playing by ear is to know which chords belong together in each key and to listen carefully so that you can hear when a chord needs to be changed, and if a chord does or does not fit with the melody. Study Figure F. It shows the basic chords for the most common major keys. The three major chords in every major key are the ones most often used in many songs. Using those three chords, you can figure out most simple songs by ear. Using the chord chart, you can see that in the key of C, the three major chords are C (I), F (IV) and G (V). In the key of G, they are G (I), C (IV) and D (V).

First, let's figure out the song *Polly Wolly Doodle* by ear in the key of G. It uses only two chords; the I chord (G) and the V chord (D). Most songs begin and end with the I chord in the key the song was written in. You will, therefore, begin the song with the I chord which is G. To help you hear the right note to begin singing with, strum the I, IV, then V chords (G, C, then D). Then begin singing the song and strumming the I chord. You will know it is time to change chords when your singing does not sound good with the chord you are playing. Since you are using only two chords, you will simply change back and forth from the G and D chords throughout the song. Other two-chord (I, V) songs are: *Go Tell Aunt Rhody, Ten Little Indians, Tom Dooley,* and *London Bridge.*

Now let's try a three chord song, *On Top Of Old Smoky,* in the key of C. The empty circles above the words show where the chord changes occur. Write the correct chords inside those circles. You will begin the song with the I chord which is C. When you get to the word "Smoky" you will need to change chords. Since the three major chords in the key of C are C, F and G (or G7), you can change to either F or G. Try them both to see which one fits. When you get to the word "snow" you will hear another need for a chord change. Again you will have two choices, and so on throughout the song (see answer below*). Other three major chord songs are: *The Camptown Races, Silent Night, Goodnight Ladies,* and *Amazing Grace.*

ON TOP OF OLD SMOKY

Chords: C, G7, F

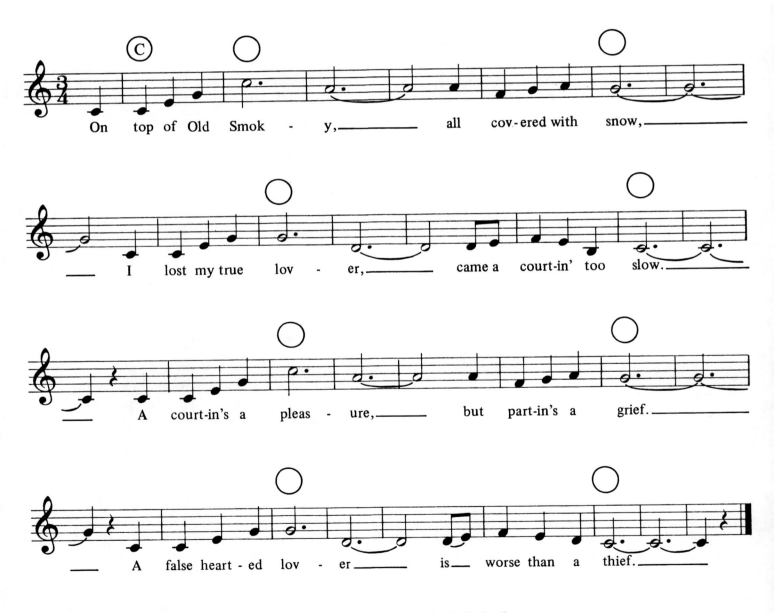

*The chords for *On Top Of Old Smoky* are as follows: C, F, C, G, C, F, C, G, C.

Minor chords can add *color* to a song written in a major key. Below are two versions of *Michael Row The Boat Ashore* in the key of F. The first version is arranged with all major chords (I, IV, V). The second version also uses the ii and iii chords, G minor and A minor. Can you hear where those minor chords belong and write them in the empty circles below?**

MICHAEL, ROW THE BOAT ASHORE

VERSION 1:

2. Sister, help to trim the sails, hallelujah.
Sister, help to trim the sails, hallelujah.

3. River Jordan is chilly and cold, hallelujah.
Chills the body but not the soul, hallelujah.

VERSION 2:

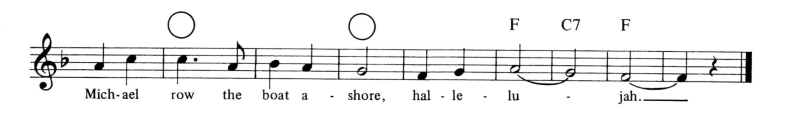

**A minor above "row" and G minor above "shore."

Appendix B: Care and Maintenance of the Autoharp

TUNING

Tuning thirty-six strings may seem hard at first, but with practice you can learn to tune easily. You will need a few tools before you can begin. You will need a *pitch reference,* a source by which you can check the pitch of your Autoharp. Many beginners use a chromatic pitch pipe, which is quite inexpensive and offers a reasonably accurate scale from middle C through high C. You may also tune your instrument to a piano. In addition, you will need a tuning tool to adjust the strings. I recommend a harpsichord tuner instead of the regular Autoharp tuner because it is longer, gives better leverage, and makes the Autoharp pegs slightly more responsive to your touch. Unfortunately, the pegs are not very sensitive; sometimes they will seem stiff and at other times, the slightest movement of the tuner will set the string very sharp or flat. You can compensate by moving the tuner slowly and carefully; train yourself to hear subtle differences in pitch.

To begin tuning, lay the Autoharp on a flat and stable surface. Choose one note, A, for example, and tune all the A's first. Then moving up the scale chromatically, tune all the A♯'s, all the B's, all the C's, and so on. The palm of your left hand steadies the Autoharp. Your right thumb strikes the strings to be tuned. The right hand also turns the tuner.

Suppose you have decided to start by tuning your A strings. Put your tuner on the highest A peg. Play the high A on your pitch source and strike the high A on your Autoharp. Listen carefully for differences in the two sounds. Listen for a *beating* of the vibrations which you will want to adjust until you hear only a clear tone. By turning the tuning peg you will be able to get the vibrations of the two sounds synchronized. Once you get the high A in tune, it becomes your reference note. Strike the reference note first and tune the next lower A on the Autoharp to it. When the next A is in tune, it becomes the reference note for the next lower A, and so on.

Here are a few hints you may find helpful:

• If a note is just slightly sharp, it may be more effective to press down on the string with your finger than to turn the peg.

• Turn the peg only as long as you hear both notes ringing, and when vibrations begin to die, strike each note again.

• Try using one finger from your left hand to mark the string to be tuned, by resting it on the string just below it (for A, your finger would rest on the G♯). This prevents frantic moments searching for the second note while your reference note fades away.

• The strings on a new Autoharp have to go through an initial stretching period before they will hold their pitch. They will need to be tuned perhaps three to five times at various intervals before the new strings adjust. You can stretch a string more quickly by pulling it up firmly with your fingers. When you release it, you will notice that it has gone down in pitch. Tune it back up to pitch and pull on it again. Release and tune. Repeat this process until the string holds its pitch.

Once the Autoharp is in tune, it should hold pitch fairly well. Each time you play you will need to check the tuning and make minor adjustments. To do this, press down a chord bar and run your finger slowly over the strings, sounding each note separately and listening for notes that sound out of tune in that chord. When you hear a note that is out of tune, stop there. Strike the same note an octave higher (or lower) and tune the note that is out of tune to it. Repeat this procedure with several other chords.

Many things can affect the strings and put the Autoharp out of tune. When you are holding the instrument make sure it does not bang against anything, as this can jar the pegs and loosen some strings. Lay it down slowly and carefully when you are finished playing. Keep it in a safe place, preferably in a case. Handle the instrument in its case as you would out of it. Never lay the case upside down as this causes the chord bars to press against the strings and puts them out of tune. Cold weather can affect the strings. During the winter months never take your Autoharp outside without having it in a case and then only for as short a period of time as possible. If it has been in the cold for any length of time, do not immediately open the case when you are inside again. Wait awhile (approximately one-half hour or so) to let the air inside the case slowly change its temperature. Also be careful not to expose your Autoharp to the direct summer sun for very long. When the instrument is at home, keep it in a place where it will not be exposed to direct cold or heat of any kind.

STRINGING

Strings need to be changed when they break or sound *dead*. The process is relatively simple and you need only to look at your Autoharp to see how it is done. However, there are still some things that you should know beforehand. There are not many music stores that carry Autoharp strings. They can often be found at folk music stores, however. Strings are made with either a *ball* or *loop* end. Check to see which type your Autoharp needs. If you are not sure, bring the old string with you when you buy the new one. Strings are sold in four octaves: high, middle, low and bass. Make sure you are buying the string in the right octave.

When you remove the old broken string, unwind the peg three or four times counter-clockwise. This will prevent the peg from being rewound too far into the instrument and thus stripping the threads in the wood. As you place the new string into the peg hole, leave enough slack so that it will wind around the peg approximately three or more times. Make sure the string winds below the peg hole and that the string is always touching itself as it winds around the peg. A new string will need to be stretched and, as stated before, this is done by pulling it up firmly with your fingers; then release it and tune. Repeat several times until the string holds its pitch. The lower octave A♭ string is notorious for not holding its pitch well. Try putting on a wound A string in place of the unwound A♭.

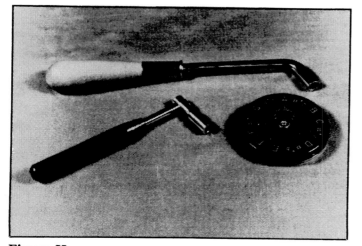

Figure H.

Figure I.

Care and Maintenance

CLEANING

Keeping your Autoharp clean preserves the wood and helps it to sound better and last longer. To clean the strings, dampen a cloth with a moderate amount of rubbing alcohol and rub vigorously up and down each string. This will remove oxidation, perspiration and oils. To clean and dust the wood, take a slightly damp cloth that is longer than the width of the Autoharp and with a flat ruler push the cloth underneath the strings. As it reaches the other side, grasp the cloth with your fingers and remove the ruler. Then, holding each end of the cloth, move it back and forth and up and down the length of the Autoharp (Figure J). Naptha is a good cleaning substance to use; it will not damage the wood and it also takes off any greasy or sticky substance. Also, if you want to polish the wood, use the same process as above with a moderate amount of guitar polish.

REFLECTING

When the felts on a chord bar become worn, notes that are not in the chord will sound, resulting in an unpleasant sounding chord. It then becomes time to replace the felt. Once you have refelted a chord bar, you will realize what a simple process it is. You can purchase felt at a folk music store in strips two feet long. Follow these instructions: Remove the bar carriage top and take out the chord bar. With a felt tip pen, mark the place on the chord bar where the old felt is attached (Figure K-1). Remove the old felt with a one-sided razor. Cut new pieces of felt the same length as the old pieces. Attach the new felt pieces to the bar by peeling off

the paper backing and pressing the sticky side onto the bar where it is marked (Figure K-2).

If you are interested in making your instrument more versatile, you may want to make some entirely new chord bars. If so, cut a strip of felt the length of your chord bar. Attach the new strip to the chord bar. Place the chord bar in the end slot of the bar carriage and push it down. Mark the contact point of string to felt for each note in the desired chord (Figure L-1). To allow for inherent play in the chord bars, push the bar down and to the right and mark the felt for the note; then push the bar down and to the left and mark the felt. The two marked spaces should be approximately one-quarter inch wide (Figure L-2). At the marks, cut the felt straight down to the metal bar and then remove the felt slices (Figure L-3). This will give you the new chord bar.

You can also modify a chord bar. For example, in changing an A7 chord to a A major chord, simply dampen the seventh note (G) in that chord. To do this cut an eighth-inch piece of felt and place it against the bar where it will dampen the G note.

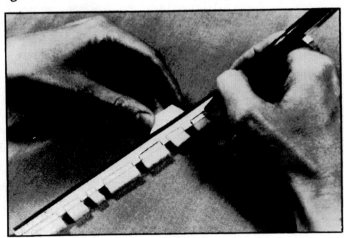

Figure K-1.

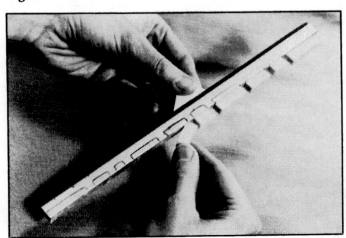

Figure K-2.

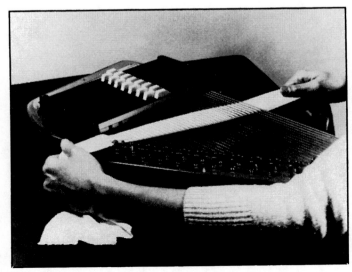

Figure J.

Figure L-1.

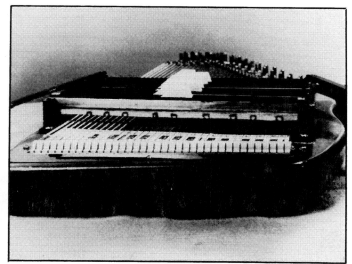

Figure L-2.

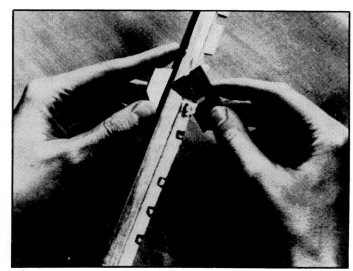

Figure L-3.

To work on your own chord bars you need to know the notes in the desired chords. Below is a chart showing the notes in the chords that are most frequently used with the Autoharp:

CHORD	NOTES IN THE CHORD			CHORD	NOTES IN THE CHORD		
F maj.	F	A	C	A min.	A	C	E
C maj.	C	E	G	D min.	D	F	A
G maj.	G	B	D	E min.	E	G	B
D maj.	D	F♯	A	G min.	G	B	D
A maj.	A	C♯	E	B min.	B	D	F♯
E maj.	E	C♯	B	F♯ min.	F♯	A	C♯
B♭ maj.	B♭	D	F	C♯ min.	C♯	E	G♯
E♭ maj.	E♭	G	B♭	G♯ min.	G♯	B	D♯
B maj.	B	D♯	F♯				
F7	F	A	C	E♭			
C7	C	E	G	B♭			
G7	G	B	D	F			
D7	D	F♯	A	C			
A7	A	C♯	E	G			
E7	E	G♯	B	D			
B♭7	B♭	D	F	A♭			
B7	B	D♯	F♯	A			

ORDERING PARTS

If you cannot find the materials you need at the music store, you can order direct from the company that builds Autoharps. Write to Fretted Industries as listed below and request their catalogs.

Fretted Industries
1415 Waukegan Road
Chicago, Illinois 60062

Selected Discography

●Neriah and Kenneth Bennfield,
Kilby Snow, Ernest Stoneman
*Mountain Music Played
On The Autoharp*
Folkways Records 2365

Evo Bluestein (& The Bluestein
Family)
Sowin' On The Mountain
Fretless Records SR 141

Andrew F. Boarman
Mountain State Music
June Appal Records 025

●Bryan Bowers
The View From Home
Flying Fish Records 037

Home, Home On The Road
Flying Fish Records 091

Maybelle Carter
Mother Maybelle Carter
Columbia Records CG 32436

Bill Clifton
Come By The Hills
Country Records 751

Another Happy Day
Country Records 758

●Patrick Couton
Autoharp Ce Soir
Iris Records TR 1012

Lindsay Haisley
*Lindsay Haisley Live At
The Kerville Folk Festival*
Gazebo Records

Clayton S. Jones
Traditional Autoharp

Sunny Mountain Records
EB 1006

John McCutcheon
How Can I Keep From Singing
June Appal Records 003

●Bonnie Phipps
Autoharpin'
Kicking Mule Records KM228

John Sebastian
(on Randy Van Warmers
Single Records)
Just When I Needed You Most
Bearsville Records BSS 0334

Mike Seegar
Old Time Country Music
Folkways Records 2325

New Lost City Ramblers, Vol. 4
Folkways Records 2399

●Kilby Snow
America
Folkways Records 3902

●Michael Stanwood,
Fingers Akimbo
Cowtowns & Other Planets
Biscuit City Records 1319

Gove Strivenor
Shady Gove
Flying Fish Records 048

Coconut Gove
Flying Fish Records 084

●Highly recommended

Autoharp Songbooks

Autoharp Anthology; MCA/Mills — 1976

   Pop Classics: 27 Hits Of Our Time

   Nostalgia: 27 Oldies But Goodies

Autoharp Songbook; Mel Bay Publications — 1981

Autoharp Parade;
Oscar Schmidt International, Inc. — 1966

   Vol. 1 — 100 Favorite Songs For Young People

   Vol. 2 — 100 World's Best Loved Songs

   Vol. 3 — 100 Hymns and Spirituals

Chords and Starts For Guitar And Autoharp,
A Collection of Children's Songs;
Colgin Publishing Company,
Box 303-CA, Manlius, New York 13104

Harp! The Herald Angels Sing! by Becky Blackley;
Oscar Schmidt International, Inc. — 1982

Hymns For The Autoharp; Mel Bay Publications — 1978

John Denver's Greatest Hits;
Cherry Lane Music Co. 1977

More Songs For The Autoharp;
Mel Bay Publications — 1981

Sesame Street Songbook;
Warner Brothers Publications, Inc. — 1970

Songs of Christmas For The Autoharp;
Mel Bay Publications — 1980

The Beatles' Greatest Hits;
Cherry Lane Music Co. — 1979

The Youngheart Autoharp Songbook (Children's Songs)
by Greg Scelsa and Steve Millang;
Oscar Schmidt International Inc. — 1982